Close to the Wind

The story of a youth group
that bought a ship

MAURICE VITTY

DEDICATED TO

Captain Denys Collins, Janice Chard,
John Luft, and Nigel Henderson, all
part of the Seacare Family and already
promoted to glory.

With thanks to

The original CCP team in Essex who stood with
us; the members of the community in Woolwich;
and, of course, the Seacare team: Simon and
Jan, John and Julie, Paul M and Adam C who
stepped out in faith with us for the ship.

Those who encouraged and guided me in the
writing of this book–Joe Laycock and Jenny
Page amongst others.

Especially though, the hundreds of prayer
partners. You astounded us with your faith,
prayers, and generosity. You taught me so
much, and it was worth doing this project just to
know how many unsung heroes there are in the
church. Thank you.

Thank you, Maurice. It is a privilege to write the foreword and a greater privilege to have known you and Hilary. May all who read this faith manual be inspired in faith and good works.

Roger. T. Forster
London, England
Leader and Founder of Ichthus Christian Fellowship
Vice President of Tearfund
Previous Chairman of The Evangelical Alliance
Co-founder of March for Jesus

INTRODUCTION

Jimmy Kendal later apologised for not taking it seriously. Ian Salter just thought I had lost the plot. He would have been right but for one thing: I knew God had spoken to me. It wasn't a sort of maverick, "the Lord has told me" that many unaccountable individuals use to justify their outrageous behaviour. No, this was born out of tears and being in tune with the heart of God on one particular matter at least, a heart broken with compassion for the Vietnamese boat people, who were fleeing Vietnam on makeshift rafts and boats, only for many of them to lose their lives in the South China Seas or at the hands of merciless pirates. Nevertheless, it must have been a shock to everyone in our communal home, the Tin Lanh (Vietnamese for "good news") Centre, when I announced it at breakfast. So what had God told me?

In a nutshell, He wanted my wife and me to sell our house and buy a ship that could be used to go to the South China Seas and rescue the boat people. In fact, He had told me this several years before, but He had also told me in accordance with Scripture to keep quiet about the vision until the appointed time (Hab. 2:3). In fact, my wife, Hilary and I shared it only with our good friends Ray and June Harvey, whom we knew would understand, as they themselves had been led to do some pretty unusual things. I should point out that my wife is an exceptional person, who instead of calling her lawyer took this calling from God very seriously. Years before, she had prayed that whatever happened in her life she wouldn't end up in a rut or, as Billy Graham puts it, a long shallow grave. Be careful what you pray for!

This is the story, then, of the Mission Seacare and the ship M.V. *Redeemer.* (M.V. stands for motor vessel and not my name, as one person thought for many years.) It is the true account of what was a remarkable chapter in the lives of myself and Hilary and all the friends who joined us and the thousands who prayed and gave money without ever being asked. Really, though, it is not about us at all; it's about a testimony to our amazing God and what He can do through ordinary people like you and me, often in spite of who we are, rather than because of who we are. I truly hope you will be encouraged by it and inspired. More than anything, I hope you will come away with renewed vision of our awesome God and an understanding that there is nothing better you can do than lay down your life for Him, wherever it may take you. The centre of His will for your life is the safest and most exciting place on earth.

Maurice Vitty
London, England

PART ONE

PLAN A

Chapter One

THE BOAT PEOPLE (SOUTH CHINA SEAS)

"The Spirit of the Lord is upon me, because the Lord has anointed Me – to preach good news to the poor, to bind the broken-hearted, to proclaim liberty to the captives." (Isaiah 61:1)

When we stepped off the plane in Bangkok, the heat was overwhelming. I was used to it really, as I had spent many years as a deck officer in the merchant navy and had travelled the world, but it was new for Hilary. Operation Mobilisation had sent Andreas, a German brother, and one of the crew of their mission ship, M. V. *Logos,* to meet us, and we embarked on a long, sweaty journey to the docks and our first marital home. What we saw next was to change our lives forever.

The Christian mission ship *Logos* had rescued ninety-three Vietnamese boat people from the South China Sea, and they were now camped out on the poop deck at the stern (back) of the ship. The *Logos* had been refused permission to leave Bangkok until another government agreed to accept these refugees into their country. The *Logos* was British-owned but registered in Singapore, and each nation thought the other one should take these people. The wrangling went on for a couple of months before Britain eventually agreed to accept them.

For two months, then, we had the privilege of getting to know these remarkable people and hearing their stories. We ate with them, played with the children, laughed and cried with them. Many gave their lives to Jesus because they had promised Him that if He saved them, that's what they would do. Being rescued by a Christian ship with a volunteer crew of 140 believers from almost every nation in the world doesn't leave much room for doubt that God heard them. At the time we didn't know that many of these Vietnamese would become long-term friends, especially little Ming, a cheeky young chap of about ten who became almost like our own son. We had endless hours of fun teaching them English. I will never forget Ming's renditions of "How are you? "Fine, thank you, and you?"

The hardest part of this period was hearing all the stories of pirate attacks on the defenceless boat people.

the Pacific coast of the Philippines. Unfortunately, the engine broke down when we were about three miles out at sea watching dolphins. We managed to row it to a remote island, which was extremely primitive by Western standards, but the locals were lovely and helped us fix our engine. They also guided us back to the mainland as night was falling. Hilary left them her Bible as a thank-you gift, and we often wonder if they ever read it and what happened to them.

The plight of the Vietnamese was always on our minds, and we made a point of visiting the Hawkins Road refugee camp in Singapore. We didn't know it then, but it was to be the first of many such visits. A branch of our mission would eventually have a base at nearby Marsiling, close to the causeway across to Malaysia.

After we had been on the *Logos* about six months, we sailed into the majestic harbour of Hong Kong, from where we were due to fly home. We would now have to say good-bye to many wonderful friends we had made, many of whom we were destined to keep in touch with. I remember dragging Hilary out of bed at 4 a.m. to join me on the bridge and witness the wonderful view of Hong Kong harbour, spectacularly lit up, a sight neither of us will ever forget.

Before we left Hong Kong, we visited the Kowloon Walled City, a huge slum area full of drug addicts, prostitutes, pimps, and gangsters. I was tempted to call it a godforsaken place, but of course it wasn't. God had plans for the walled city and had called a nineteen-year-old girl named Jackie Pullinger to simply get on a ship and get off when He told her. She got off in Hong Kong, and the rest, as they say, is history. (You can read the full, remarkable account of all that happened and is still happening in Jackie's book *Chasing the Dragon*, published by Hodder and Stoughton.) If we had learnt anything in these six months, it was that God's heart really is for the poor, the downtrodden, the lost, the broken, and the marginalised, and we could do nothing better in our lives than join Him in what He wants to do for them.

As the plane lifted high above Hong Kong, we wondered if our adventures were over. Had we had our gap year? What did the future hold? Had I really heard God speak, or was I just caught up in the emotion of it all, as many would later suggest? Well, we reasoned, we would soon find out.

Our good friend Ming, age ten

The boat people rescued by the *Logos*

The island in the Philippines where Hilary handed over her Bible.
Mount Mayon, an active volcano, is seen here in the background.

Chapter Two

THE FOUNDING OF CHRISTIAN CARE PROJECTS (CCP)

"Seek ye first the kingdom of God and His righteousness and all these things shall be added unto you." (Matthew 6:33)

We arrived back in the UK with just ten pounds in our pockets. We didn't have a home or any savings, but we were learning to trust in God for our needs; and in the years to come, this would take us on an adventure in faith that was just amazing and a real testimony to a faithful God. We also had the most incredible church behind us in Grays Baptist Tabernacle, and our friends Phillip and Judith Lisgarten invited us to live with them until we found our own place. Within a couple of days, however, we had both found employment. Hilary started work as a supply teacher, and I got a job working in a children's home. Don't ask me how!

find this polarisation in the Bible, and it seems foolish now. Yet, the only other people we came across who saw it as we did were the Ichthus Christian Fellowship, a church we would have much to do with in the future.

One of the things that bothered the Vietnamese was that many had been split up from members of their family. Even some parents had lost contact with their children, having sent them out on earlier boats with relatives before following later. Were these children even still alive? If they were, they must still be in one of the many refugee camps scattered around Southeast Asia. Hilary and I collated the names of missing relatives and children and tried to trace them through the United Nations High Commissioner for Refugees (UNHCR). Several of the missing children were from people we were visiting, like the lady in South Ockendon, who hadn't seen her son, Do Khanh Duy, for nearly four years. She now had another child her son hadn't seen at all. However, all our efforts were unsuccessful, and so we began to pray about going back to Asia ourselves to search for them.

This, of course, would be a whole new ball game for us. The last time we went out, yes, we were trusting in God, but there was a huge organisation between us and God, with people who met us at the airport and accommodated and fed us. This time that wouldn't be the case. It would be just us and God, but we knew that would be all right, even if a little daunting, and of course we had to go.

It was to be another six months before we went to Asia again. Before that, we were led to move from Grays to Southeast London, which had the biggest concentration of resettled refugees in the country in places like Thamesmead and Deptford. Along with our friend Jimmy Kendal, we bought a seven-bedroom house in Woolwich. The idea was that this would become a Christian community, housing our team, an outreach centre, and a refuge for refugees if they needed it. At its busiest it would have twenty-four living there. At times life got a little messy in Woolwich. Once a national charity asked us to hide a Vietnamese woman and her child for a couple of days. She was fleeing a violent husband who had discovered her safe house in the Midlands. We agreed, but the charity soon forgot about her and us. Eventually the husband found her and came down with some heavies to kidnap the baby back. A tug of war through the front window ensued, and the police were called and eventually sorted it all out.

We moved to St. Mildreds Church in Lee at this time, which again was the leading of God, as this congregation was just amazing in the way they supported us. They asked us to take on the youth work, which we did. We took the youngsters out regularly to do evangelism, which they loved, especially when Simon Kreitem set his drum kit up on the local estates and let the kids have a go. Later, this very youth group would become the core team of the Seacare project and the first crew of the *Redeemer,* amazingly with the backing of the whole church and their parents.

This was an exciting time to be a Christian. Billy Graham was in the UK for Mission England, and Luis Palau was here for Mission to London, and we threw ourselves into both. We met and made friends with many leaders and evangelists at that time, including Roger and Faith Forster, Roger and Sue Mitchell, Ray Mayhew, Clive Calver, and Eric Delve, and we even got a lengthy time to chat with Luis Palau, who impressed me immensely. I worked as a counsellor at the Blackheath Mission and as a coordinator of the team at the QPR stadium, which was invaded by activists every night, intent on causing trouble and storming the pitch every time there was an altar call. I never expected that doing rugby tackles would be a requirement of the job, but Luis was in real danger, and so we all had to act. Bringing someone down "in love" and then sharing the gospel was very interesting. Of course we were able to take the Vietnamese to these meetings too, and a real highlight was taking Ming, now resettled in Erdington, Birmingham, to hear Billy Graham at the Aston Villa stadium.

Our community, now called the Tin Lanh (Vietnamese for "good news") Centre was ticking over nicely. Our team now consisted of Simon Kreitem, Janice Trowell,

John Church, Paul Milligan, and Julie Annan from the St. Mildreds youth group, and we had various people from Ichthus stay with us too. In fact, the outreach at that time into the local community later seemed to form the nucleus of a new Ichthus congregation in Woolwich.

At the same time, the Essex team continued to reach out to the refugees housed along the northern side of the Thames from Southend to South Ockendon.

Friday night became the Bible study and prayer time, which sometimes went on all night or occasionally stopped about 2 a.m., when we would go out and seek to reach those coming out of the clubs. Also at that time we set up Streetcare as a second Christian Care Project. Living in London means you come across many needs, and this was an outreach to the homeless sleepers in places like Cardboard City (now the IMAX cinema at Waterloo), Lincolns Inn Fields, and in the network of subway tunnels at Hyde Park Corner. We used to go out about ten o'clock at night and stay out until about 4 a.m. We didn't just distribute food but stayed and chatted with individuals, often for hours. Sometimes we just listened, and sometimes we prayed with them. The main thing was that they knew we cared and therefore knew God cared.

All the time, though, the thought of Vietnamese children stuck in refugee camps in Asia, not knowing if their parents were alive and vice versa, was never far from our minds. Also, the boat people were continuing

Chapter Three

THAILAND, MALAYSIA, SINGAPORE, AND INDONESIA

"The type of fast I require is to spend yourselves on the poor and feed the hungry, set the captives free … then I will strengthen your frame in a sun parched land … and your light will break forth like the dawn." (Isaiah 58)

Once again Bangkok was the first port of call, and this time there was no one to meet us. We stayed for two days in a guesthouse run by the Overseas Missionary Fellowship, which helped us get our bearings. The plan was to visit as many camps as we could in Thailand, Malaysia, Singapore, and, if possible, Indonesia. We had also promised our Laotian friends living in Southend that we would attempt to get into Laos and visit their parents, though it seemed improbable, as it was a closed country.

First stop, then, was Nong Khai on the banks of the Mekong River directly opposite the capital of Laos, Vientiane, and we travelled there by train. As we suspected, it was impossible to cross the river into Laos, even though we investigated several options. We probably could have done it if we hadn't minded spending the rest of our lives in a Laotian jail. Our trip wasn't wasted, though, as we visited the nearby refugee camp, which was full of Laotians, including some who knew our friends. We met and made new friends here and gave out Gideon Bibles that had Laotian on one side of the page and English on the other. What better way to learn English? From here the plan was to head to Ban Vinai in the direction of Burma, and the only way was by bus.

The top speed of this bus seemed to be about 10 miles per hour, and it was full of tribal people with red teeth chewing on sticks. Every couple of miles there were roadblocks, and scary looking men in uniforms with machine guns came on board. We noticed, too, that everywhere there seemed to be signs with skulls and crossbones on them and something written in Thai. We were glad we had a friend waiting for us at Ban Vinai. Our German friend Wolfgang had been with us on the OM ship *Logos* and was now working with Southeast Asian Outreach in a camp at Ban Vinai. We would stay with Wolfgang and the team several days, just long really tough, but now it was all worth it for this was truly a wonderful moment.

All the children were just as important, of course, but this was a family we had a special bond with and was the human face of all those missing we were trying to find. All in all, we found all the children we were looking for except for one. The one we didn't find was the ten-year-old daughter of a family in Canada. It was one of the worst moments of my life to have to report to them our lack of success.

We continued on by train to Singapore and stayed with our good friends, Linda and Boon Beng Chia. We had met them while we were visiting some Vietnamese in Leeds, where they were studying at University. Boon Beng was in the navy, and they lived in a military com-plex, which, compared to what we had been used to, was luxurious and even had a swimming pool. We had sent a huge box of Bibles and cassette tapes ahead of us to the OM headquarters; and armed with these, we set off for the refugee camp at Hawkins Road. Here we met the Reverend Philip Tan, who became a great friend and later set up a CCP base in nearby Marsiling. Philip really had a heart for the poor; and in a culture where many were seeking fame and recognition, he was content to humbly serve behind the scenes in the refugee camp and in the notorious Changi prison. Once again we made many new Vietnamese friends in the camp, and we sat for hours teaching English from our dual language Bibles and the Reverend Roy Hicks's evangelistic cassettes, which were recordings of services he had held in Vietnamese and Cantonese in a refugee holding centre near Bournemouth, England. The boat people loved it, and so did we. We were very sad to leave, but we would return again on several further occasions over the years.

Before we left Singapore, we made friends with many others, including the Canadian couple, Tom and Donna Perkins, who worked for Food For the Hungry and were presently operating a small ship out of Singapore to rescue the boat people. We learnt from them much about the pitfalls of such operations. We also met Shashi Tharoor, who headed up the UNHCR in Singapore and was a great help to us. From the UNHCR offices in a skyscraper overlooking the Singapore Straits, you could just see the Island of Pulau Bandang, the closest point of Indonesia to Singapore and the home of an even bigger refugee camp than Singapore's. I really wanted to visit this camp, as it was all a bit hush-hush and not a lot was known about it. Indonesia, though, was a tricky place to get into.

Once again I had to follow a bureaucratic paper trail, and again and again it looked like it was going to be impossible to go. Shashi, though, was keen for Westerners to see the situation in these camps; and after he pulled a few strings, the door was opened and permission was granted. This time I went on my own and left Hilary with Boon Beng and Linda. I had been to a port on a nearby island years before when I was in the merchant navy, and I remembered it as a really scary and dodgy place. I travelled to the island by boat from Singapore and once there managed to find a room in the only hotel in town. Actually, it was more like a youth hostel, but it was good enough for my needs.

Once again it seemed to be me that I benefited more from these visits than the refugees, as again I was given food and drink and basically just humbled by the way the Vietnamese conducted themselves. That said, the refugees themselves wouldn't agree. Again and again they would say, "Thank you for coming." Even though I achieved very little, they were grateful not to be forgotten. These thoughts again would sustain me during times of criticism. It's hard to believe that wanting to help others should trigger so much hostility in some people, and it was just a few; but we had constantly been told things like, "You won't achieve anything," "Leave it to the long-term workers," and "Anything you do will just be a drop in the ocean." I had an answer for the last one because I remember what Mother Theresa used to reply: "The ocean is made up of drops."

We weren't quite finished in Southeast Asia. We had one more stop in our search for missing children, and that was Songkla in southern Thailand. We took the Singapore-to-Bangkok train again but got off in Hat Yai, a town in the centre of the southern part of Thailand.

From here we had to get a bus. We had been told this was an area known for bandits and was probably where the "pirates" lived. Just a couple of weeks earlier, it had been on the news that over a hundred decomposed bodies of Vietnamese boat people had washed up on the beach at Songkla. It was on that beach we now stood and prayed. We had checked out the camp at Songkla but didn't find any more of the children. We feared the worst for the daughter of the family in Canada. Now on the beach, with that picture of bodies in our minds, the tears flowed, and we talked to God. Now was the time to go for the ship. Now was the time to tell everyone what God had put in our hearts to do. Surely many would think we were out of our minds and some would judge our motives, but God was preparing many more to stand with us and believe. The Bible says that the work of God is to believe in Him who was sent (John 6:29), for it is not a work we do for Him but something He does through us. I was scared to go public with the vision of the ship, but on that beach the sense of urgency was never stronger, and God gave us the green light. He did more than that; He told us to prepare ourselves because in two years' time we would have the ship.

Exactly two years later in the Dutch port of Den Oever, the Special Service ship *Castor* was sold to a handful of youngsters, the youth group of St Mildred's Church in Lee, Southeast London, who basically made up our team. We renamed the ship *Redeemer*.

50

Hilary with the children in Sungei Besi Camp near Kuala Lumpur

Maurice at Sungei Besi

Do Khanh Duy reunited at Heathrow Airport with his
mother and the brother he had never met

The Truong Family, who would soon live with us
in Woolwich

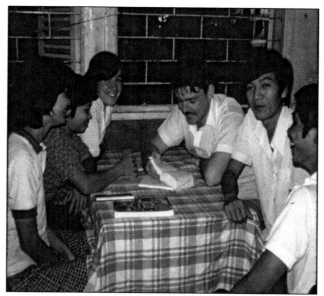

Teaching English in the Hawkins Road Camp
in Singapore

Looking over the Mekong River into Laos

With Wolfgang Hable at Ban Vinai towards Burma, where we met
the Hmong hill tribes

Chapter Four

MINNESOTA, USA

"Sanctify yourselves, for tomorrow the Lord will do wonders amongst you." (Joshua 3:5)

W hat did the Lord mean by telling us to prepare ourselves? Surely there was much work to be done, infrastructure to put in place. Where do you start with something like this? In the end that infrastructure would involve having a charity in the UK and a nonprofit organisation in the USA. It would involve setting up various companies, two of them shipping companies, one in Britain and one in Malta. It would involve registering a ship under the flag of St. Vincent and the Grenadines in the Caribbean, though their office was in Monaco, and using a French classification society, called Bureau Veritas. There would be offices or representatives in Britain, Holland, America, and Singapore and numerous bank accounts in all these places. Yet God had said simply, "Prepare yourselves."

Verses of Scripture came to mind: "Unless the Lord builds the house the labourers labour in vain" (Psalm 127:1) and "Not by might nor by power, but by My Spirit says the Lord" (Zechariah 4:6). It was clear that this wasn't something we were going to do for God but something He was going to do through us, if we would believe and create the conditions for His Spirit to come and work. So what were we to do? The answer was clear: we were to take a year out and go to Bible College. "OK, Lord," we thought, "but where?" We assumed—wrongly—that it would be one of the many excellent colleges in the UK; but, no, we were sure He was directing us to the United States of America and not to one of the well-known places but to a tiny, obscure little place in northern Minnesota called Bemidji. The Lord sure does work in mysterious ways.

By this time we had been blessed with our first child, Sarah, and shooting off to America didn't seem such a good idea. We also knew we would need the green light from our trustees and our local church elders. This is an important biblical principle that we always followed as a safeguard to getting carried away with our own fanciful ideas. However, we were in for a shock, as our church elders said no; they didn't think it was God's will for us to go. We, of course, were sure that it was, so our biblical principle of submission was really going to be put to the test.

It's no use throwing out your principles when they don't go your way, however, so we knew we would have to submit to this; and we did. However, at the same time God was speaking to our elders, who came back to us two weeks later and said that after further prayer and reflection they now believed God did want us to go.

In August, then, we flew out to New York with baby Sarah too. We hired a car and drove up to Toronto, where we visited a Vietnamese girl who had been rescued by the *Logos*. From there we went on to London, Ontario, where we visited another Vietnamese family rescued by the *Logos* and our old neighbours from Grays, Mike and Janet Williamson, who now lived there too. From here we drove on through Canada, eventually dropping back into the States in Milwaukee before continuing on to Bemidji.

You never expect a culture shock so much in the States because there is so much we have in common. However in the Midwest people are very conservative, and it was really strange at first. That said, the people were so friendly and so welcoming that it was to be one of the best years of our lives. Temperatures of -40°C were interesting. You could buy a frozen chicken and leave it in the boot (trunk) of your car if you liked. In fact, you had to plug your car into the electric overnight to stop the oil from getting too thick, and you never went out with your hair wet! An emergency survival kit in the car was a must in case of breakdown.

We didn't tell anyone in Bemidji about our plans for the ship until the last few weeks we were there, preferring instead to do as the Lord had said and prepare ourselves personally. This meant getting in shape spiritually and physically. I lost two stone before we returned to England, largely due, I think, to the part-time job I had of chopping wood.

In Minnesota the summers are hot. I got the worst sunburn of my life when I went on a canoe trip down the Mississippi. Yet in winter you can drive your car over frozen lakes, which we did regularly. The fall, of course, is awesome with such amazing colours. Another fond memory was seeing the northern lights, and yet another was cross-country skiing. This was certainly a world away from Southeast London.

More important than all of this, of course, was the making of new friendships that would last a lifetime and become an integral part of Seacare, a nonprofit organisation that eventually would be set up in Bemidji with its own board of directors, and would bring a steady stream of people out to the ship. Not least among these was Adam Charon, who was with us almost from day one when we joined the ship in Holland.

The Lord was still teaching us much about faith, and I was soon to write a book on the subject with Adam's help. One amazing lesson I learnt was when my good friend Jim Meehan invited me to the Full Gospel Business Men's Breakfast in a local restaurant. In the UK they are normally dinners, but the Americans love breakfast and what at first seemed to us as awful—mixing sizzle sausages, scrambled eggs, pancakes, and maple syrup together on the same plate—became a favourite, often enjoyed by us today in Southeast London. The speaker at this meeting was a missionary, and it was decided by Jim to take up an offering for him. I, as a poor student, had only enough to pay for my breakfast, but I felt the Lord telling me to put what I had in the offering. This didn't seem right and was probably irresponsible and reckless, except that I had thought the Lord had prompted me; so that's what I did. At the end of the meeting, the waitress was coming around to us all in turn to collect the money for our food. As she got closer to me, I felt very foolish and embarrassed about my predicament. However, when she got to me, she said, "Oh you don't have to pay. Somebody else in the restaurant (she pointed to a guy I had never seen before) has paid for you." I couldn't believe it. What a way to learn about faith, or was it more obedience?

I entitled my book *Great Exploits or Trivial Pursuit* because God was challenging me about the life of Daniel, who said, "The people who know their God shall be strong and carry out great exploits" (Daniel 11:32). Also at the time the game Trivial Pursuit had just come out. What would I spend my life on? I felt God asking.

Would it be great exploits or trivial pursuits? Adam Charon kindly typed the entire manuscript for me, and I based it on the lives of all the heroes of faith mentioned in Hebrews 11.

Jim Meehan, on the other hand, helped us to set up Seacare/CCP as a nonprofit organisation in the States. Jim was joined as a director by William Dale Pederson, a lecturer at Oak Hills Bible School, and Pastor Don Stollhammer from Northern Bible Church, where Hilary and I had chosen to worship.

It was time to fly home and buy a ship.

right. Here was one of the strongest, soundest, most seaworthy ships of its size ever built. The only negative was that her fine lines, which made her beautiful to a seadog like me, would also make her roll and pitch like mad in a seaway. This was something we would soon experience because we had found our ship, and we put a deposit down.

I have some good photos of Simon and myself on the ferry back to England, looking completely spaced out with that undeniable "What have I done?" look on our faces. A combination of tremendous excitement and sheer panic just about sums it up!

A couple of weeks later, Hilary and I and our two-year-old Sarah were on our way to Holland with a team that was largely the St. Mildreds youth group. Now some churches wouldn't like that, but St. Mildreds was special. We had the blessing of everyone (as far as I know), even the parents! Quite something. The financial and prayer support that came from St. Mildreds was phenomenal, and people would later regularly fly out and visit us. Tim Chard made a six-foot-long model of the ship, and when he married Janice Petty at St. Mildreds, they said, "No gifts for us, please. If you would like to make a donation to Seacare, you can drop it into the funnel of the ship on the way out."

Once we were in Holland, it was time to roll our sleeves up and get stuck in. We were soon joined by many Dutch friends, like Kees Hulsbergen, who had been another engineer on the *Logos,* and many of Kees's friends helped too. The ship basically needed to be chipped and painted from end to end; many pipes in the engine room needed totally replacing; a lot of work needed to be done inside too. Julie was our chef and was later joined by a Dutchman called Marco, who would end up sailing with us. Adam Charon flew in from Minnesota. John Church was our engineer, a first for him, but he can turn his hand to anything. Despite all the work that was needed, we felt it would be good to set a date for departure, as this would help us focus. We decided we would sail in exactly three months. It seemed impossible, but it certainly galvanised us and got us moving. The people we had bought the ship from were on hand to help us out and show us how things worked. We knew they thought we were crazy, but we had a great time with them. They treated Simon and me to raw herring, a local delight—you have to put your head back and lower the whole thing into your mouth. We were spitting out scales for days. One of the owners had a little donkey that our Sarah was delighted with. She also was thrilled with the swing park right next to the ship. Despite the work that needed to be done, we also took time off for fun and for outreach, holding open-airs at local fun fairs.

We were just one week from our sailing date when we were delivered a massive blow. The surveyor from the French Classification Society told us that because we were over 400 gross tonnes we needed an oily water separator, a device that reduces the amount of oil down to negligible amounts so that you can pump the bilge water overboard. We wouldn't be able to sail. The locals were sympathetic and said we had given it our best shot. However, we had been telling people that with God all things are possible. Was it our pride or His reputation that was at stake?

The nearest device we could buy was in Haarlem, Kees's and Marianne's hometown, and it cost £4000. That was a huge amount then, and we didn't have anything like that. I was due back in London that day to report to the trustees before we sailed. I went straight to the meeting before going to pick up the mail and spent the night at Jan and Tim's house. To say I was disappointed would be an understatement, and the meeting was subdued. I really thought it was right to sail on that day, not least so that we could get through the Bay of Biscay before the severest winter weather set in. After the meeting I picked up the mail from our box number in Lee, Southeast London. There was a letter in it from a lady in the Home Counties. The name wasn't familiar, as it wasn't somebody on our mailing list. She said, "*The Lord woke me up in the middle of the night and told me to sell my car and give the money to Seacare.*" There was a cheque for £3000. The words *feather* and *knock me down* describe how I felt at that moment. It was incredible. The only way to thank this lady was to write to her through her bank, and to this day I don't know who she is. Immediately I was on the phone to the ship. "Get the oily water separator. We're going to sail!"

Of course it didn't just have to be bought; it had to be fitted too and in just a few days. Our Dutch friends worked flat out on it, as the surveyor was coming back immediately prior to sailing to inspect it.

Meanwhile Simon and Janice had gone back to London, where we had an office at London Bridge. The plan was to sail straight out to Southeast Asia, stopping at Malta to refuel. Simon and I began to wonder if we could fit a trip in to London on the way to give our supporters in the area a chance to visit the ship. Incidentally, we had now renamed the ship *Redeemer* (as we love to sing, the name above all names). If we could get to London, it would be too late to get the word out nationwide, as it was so last minute, but there were a huge number of supporters in the Southeast who would have opportunity to come. We decided to go for it, and I knew if anyone could make it happen, Simon could. He's just like that, and, of course, he had God on his side. It wasn't long before I got the call from Simon. Yes, we could come to London. I thought Tilbury or maybe even Canary Wharf would be something. "No," Simon said, "the Pool of London, and they will be raising Tower Bridge." Wow!

It was just hours before the deadline, and the surveyor was back on board. "You have done incredibly well to get this far, but unfortunately you haven't finished connecting it up, and it can't be tested. I am afraid I can't let you sail," he said. The Dutch guys working on it had been due to leave the ship in Holland, but they came up with a brainwave. They said to the surveyor, "Look, if we sail with the vessel, which is only going to London, we can guarantee that we will have it up and running by the time we get there, and you could send your man in London to check it."

It was a long shot. The surveyor pondered it for a while. "Ok," he said, "that sounds reasonable. I agree." A few hours later the *Redeemer* slipped her moorings and quietly sailed out into the mist, destination London. It was exactly three months to the day.

Before

And After

Chapter Six

FOR THOSE IN PERIL ON THE SEA (LONDON, PORTUGAL, MALTA)

"If your presence does not go with us, do not lead us up from here." (Exodus 33:15)

The North Sea was like a millpond. In all my years at sea, I had never seen it like this. The sea was flat calm like a mirror, and the *Redeemer* glided through it gracefully. I shouted down from the bridge wing to Adam and Simon working on deck, "This is the life!" It was something that would become a bit of a catchphrase associated with me. Yet it was the middle of winter. Was I being lulled into a false sense of security?

I began to ponder what had led me to this place. I had left my home in Scunthorpe to attend the nautical school in Hull when I was just thirteen. We all stayed in lodgings all week then on Friday afternoon got the paddle steamer (OK, I am not quite as old as Noah) back to New Holland and hitched a lift home.

I was an atheist in those days and thought I was very clever. I went to the headmaster to tell him that I shouldn't have to go into assembly because I was a humanist. "OK," he said, and from that day on I had to stay in a classroom on my own, bored stiff, whilst my mates fooled around in the assembly. I think my headmaster was even cleverer than I.

There were two nautical schools in Hull, the posh one, Trinity House, where they wore battledress for uniform and ours, the Boulevard, where we wore ordinary merchant navy uniforms and which was located in a rough part of town near the Fish Docks. We called each other "bilge," not that we understood what this nautical term meant, but it sounded pretty derogatory, and so it was fine.

Once a year the two schools came together at St. Alfred's Church in the city centre for the Seafarers Memorial Service. I remember being presented with a book called the *Shoregoers Guide to World Ports,* which I still have. I got this for coming first in an essay writing competition. The strange thing was that my essay was about Jesus returning to earth as a tramp and nobody recognising him. Where did that come from in the mind of a young humanist?

Anyway, I digress. The point of this episode is that every year at this service we would sing the hymn,

"Eternal Father Strong to Save." Perhaps you remember the chorus: "Oh hear us when we cry to thee for those in peril on the sea."

It always brought a tear to my eye, so I am not surprised now when I look back at my life and realise that the bulk of it has been committed to saving souls at sea.

I was to learn too in a very dramatic way how hazardous sea life could be. I had hoped, after my GCSEs, to go to sea with a company called Houlder Brothers. I had hoped to go on their flagship the *Royston Grange* on the run to Argentina, as this ship took passengers and lots of first-trip deck cadets like myself. However, due to a computer glitch my GCSE results were delayed, and I missed the opportunity. While I was waiting for these results, news came through that the *Royston Grange* had been in a collision with the tanker *Tin Chien* in the River Plate. The RG had ripped a large gash in the side of the tanker, which was leaking oil. The vapour of this oil totally engulfed the RG, and the grating of metal between the two ships created the inevitable spark. The RG was engulfed in a ball of flame that killed all seventy-two people aboard and ten on the *Tien Chien*. All that was found of the casualties were skeletons.

Now here I was in a tranquil North Sea, thinking about the responsibility I now had to operate a ship with a crew of untrained youngsters supported by a few professionals who often would be able to give only a few days or weeks. I was pleased we had on board the very experienced captains, Tage Benson from Sweden and Denys Collins from England. John also now had a couple of qualified Dutch engineers for part of the voyage at least.

I felt a real responsibility to these youngsters and their parents and sending churches. I also had my wife and baby daughter on board; it was all very sobering. Until now I had just been the youth leader and friend of the youngsters. Now I had to put my captain's hat on and start to run a tight and disciplined ship. Most people understood that, even though they found it difficult, because they could see for themselves the dangers. I did receive one letter, though, from somebody who visited the ship later on, slating me for being too harsh. I am sure at times I must have got it wrong, but we eventually operated for ten years with volunteers from all over the world without accident or injury (except once when Adam got some acid in his face from the radio batteries). I am proud of that record and personally think I got it about right.

We navigated up the Thames ourselves as far as Gravesend, where we had to take a pilot, who had local knowledge, to take us the rest of the way to our berth at Tower Bridge, where a large crowd had gathered for our arrival. The crowd was excited to see a chalkboard by the bridge that declared, "At 3:00 p.m. this bridge will be raised for the *Redeemer.*" And at exactly 3:00 p.m. the same message was announced on the Tannoy to lots of cheers, as my favourite bridge in all the world majestically was raised and stopped the traffic in central London.

Unfortunately, we did hit the jetty with a bit of a bump, but at least we hadn't damaged the Queen's launch. The next days were to be manic, taking stores, receiving hundreds of visitors, and giving media interviews. We were joined by Colin and Diana from Lowestoft. Colin had been a marine surveyor, and they brought us a gift, a huge RIB (rigid, inflatable boat) with an outboard motor that could seat fourteen people. It would be invaluable in the days and years ahead.

One London businessman who had heard my interview on the LBC radio station came down to give me £50 and ask for my autograph. I thought, "I don't do autographs. I am not a celebrity." But then I thought that we are always complaining about our superficial celebrity culture, and here was a man who had looked beyond that; so I gave it to him.

After three days it was time to sail. In more ways than one, we were about to learn that the party really was over. I have a lovely photograph somebody took of Simon's mum standing on the quay and watching her son sail off into the distance to an unknown future. The parents of these youngsters were very special indeed, and for me I found their trust very humbling.

We hadn't gone far before an alarm was going off in the engine room. The engine was overheating, and we would have to stop. We limped into an anchorage off Gravesend to inspect the damage. A cooler made of cast iron had cracked. It was late at night, and it would need welding and would have to go ashore. Welding cast iron is a specialist skill that not many could do. Undeterred, we decided to go ashore with it there and then. This would be the first use of the RIB, and we sneaked ashore looking like an SAS patrol. We found a remote quay and had to climb fifty feet up a vertical ladder. We were in the middle of nowhere, so we walked towards the lights and eventually found a road and flagged a taxi down. The taxi driver said, "I might be able to help you. I know somebody who does this kind of thing." He took us to a house; and despite the late hour, a man was working around the back in his workshop. "No problem!" he said. "I have the equipment, and I will do it now." In no time at all, we had it fixed and were on our way back to the ship. The engineers stayed up all night and fitted the new part. At first light we were on our way again.

We were fine until we got to Dover; but as soon as we rounded the corner into the English Channel, it was a very different matter. Our cabin was right at the forward end of the ship, and we were lying in bed when suddenly we seemed to be being lifted up about thirty feet into the air and dropped down again, and it was getting worse and worse. I got up and made my way to the bridge. A huge Atlantic swell was funnelling its way down the channel, and our vessel was pitching wildly. Pitching is when the bow comes up and down as does the stern, it's different to rolling where the ship heels over from side to side. It's like being on a fairground ride, but the novelty very quickly wears off. Our speed had reduced down to less than two knots. I remember looking out of the bridge window at Dungeness power station in the morning, and in the afternoon it seemed like it was in the same place.

I have never suffered from seasickness, but now the vast majority of my crew were very ill indeed. Most of them had to retire to the lower cabins in the vessel (where the movement wasn't so bad). Those of us who could manage were going to have to stay awake an awfully long time. Hilary had taken our two-year-old daughter, Sarah, down to a lower cabin, and I went down to see if they were OK. By now the ship was being thrown around wildly, and as I had never been on a ship as small as this, it was something I had never experienced the likes of either. I remember Sarah saying, "Daddy, will you look after me?" At that moment I am sure I sprouted my first grey hairs. Had I got it wrong? What had I done? Was this a massive error of judgement that could lead to a catastrophe? Then I remembered how clear the calling had been and how many answers to prayer there had been along the way. No, everything would be fine. God had called, and

God would protect. A peace came over me that I was hopefully able to pass on to others.

When we got into the Bay of Biscay, it was even worse, as now we were heading south and the swell was on the beam, causing us to roll from side to side really violently. It was such a relief when, after a couple of days, it calmed down a bit and we decided to put into Oporto in northern Portugal for a bit of respite. We stayed just twenty-four hours in order to get some sleep and food that would stay down. Then we were on our way again to Malta, where we would refuel for the journey on to the South China Sea.

News was coming through to us, though, of the changing situation in Vietnam. The war was over, and the boat people problem was changing too, by the hour. Where there had been a steady stream of refugees, it was now just a trickle and looked to be something that would be completely over soon. On the one hand, of course, we were thrilled. We had shed many a tear over the plight of the boat people, and nobody could be happier than we were about this news. We certainly didn't want to see the problem continue just so we could be heroes and have a ministry. However, there were many questions we now had. Had we got this wrong? What about all the people who had prayed and given generously and even joined us? What would they think? What did we think? Where would we go from here? For now they were all questions that would have to wait until we arrived in Malta. There were ten days of sailing left, and the bulk of it would be in bad weather, albeit not as extreme as what we had just come through.

We got to Malta a little early. I remember the port didn't want us until 0900 hours, so we stopped our engines just off the coast of the northernmost Maltese Island of Gozo at 0300 hours and drifted until daylight. I was flabbergasted by what I saw when the sun came up, for we were in the most turquoise-blue and crystal-clear waters I have ever seen in my life. You could easily see 60 feet or even 80 feet or 100 feet down. I instantly fell in love with the place.

Soon we had fired up our engines and were making our way past the little island of Comino and down the mainland coast to Valletta. Valletta is one of the world's greatest natural harbours, an absolutely fabulous place and one we would sail in and out of many a time over the years to come. Janice, who was training to be a nurse, had returned to London from Holland and so hadn't sailed with us. She was there now, though, in Upper Barracca Gardens, overlooking Grand Harbour and waving us in. When I say "us," I forget that she and Simon had become engaged to be married and so perhaps her thoughts were more on him.

We had made it, but we were battered and bruised. All the paint we had put on the ship in Holland had come off in the storms. The ship was a mess, we were a mess, and we were totally despondent and demoralized. We needed some time to recover.

We were confused about the way ahead. Where was God? And the storms weren't over, as Malta was about to be hit by the worst storm in living memory, a storm that would cause nearly every ship in the harbour to break its moorings and drift loose. What had we got ourselves into? Was there hope?

Whilst all this was going on, Sarah asked Mum Hilary to pray a simple prayer: "Thank you, Lord, for the swings and park in Holland. Please, could you provide the same for Sarah in Malta?" As we sailed into the very deepest part of Valletta harbour, an industrial estate with a huge coal berth, engineering workshops, and the like, it seemed highly unlikely that there would be a park anywhere; but as we came alongside and cleared the blocked view of a warehouse, there it was, a beautiful little park on a hillside just fifty yards from the ship.

God was still with us. We just needed to take stock. If plan A was no longer on, was there a plan B? We would soon find out.

We are raising the bridge for The *REDEEMER.*

A wonderful location next to the Queen's launch at Tower
Pier, central London.

But it wasn't all going
to be plain sailing.

So it was good to know we wouldn't be alone.

PART TWO

PLAN B

Chapter Seven

LANDFALL

"The island was called Malta." (Acts 28:1)

I t's hard to know where to begin with Malta. Instead of the short stopover to refuel, it became the *Redeemer's* home port for ten years. On a couple of occasions we thought we were going to follow in the apostle Paul's footsteps and be shipwrecked there, as we too had our battles with the infamous *Gregale,* the particularly bad Northeast storm that sends a huge swell surging into the harbours.

The people of Malta are wonderful, and we were made so welcome and made many new friends. Our son, Matthew, was born there, and a couple of years ago was out training with the Malta under-21 national football team. Sadly, it transpired that he was born three months too late to qualify for dual citizenship. (Sorry about that Matt! We let you down even before you were born.)

Our first period in Malta saw us helping Canadian pastor Abe Friesen to run his Full Gospel Centre. The Friesen Five—Abe, Olga, and their three children—were an amazing family. The entire Seacare team took part in services and outreach, and we saw many great things happen. Abe even trusted us to run things when he was abroad. Later we would attend and work with many other churches and become friends with many local pastors and missionaries, including Joe Fenech Laudi, Chris and Bev Gillen, Nick and Linda Attard Montalto, Edwin Caruana, and many others.

Also later we introduced March for Jesus to Malta. This movement, which became a massive, worldwide phenomenon, had been started by our friends in Ichthus and Pioneer, and we had been on the first one ever in Soho, London. The form it took in Malta was many churches coming together on the seafront at Sliema and marching to St. Julians. At the same time, we were close offshore with the ship, paralleling the route, with a huge banner up between the masts, reading, "Jesus is Lord." It was quite a sight and, though I say so myself, not a bad piece of navigation either, as we were very close in and had to be careful not to go aground.

Some of the highlights over the years were inviting Ian White and later Noel Richards to come out and take concerts. They both did this in schools, at large celebrations and conferences, etc. We even had Ian singing and witnessing at a night club. I remember he had to compete with a video of the rock band Queen performing live at Wembley Stadium, however it wasn't long before the crowd were asking for the video to be left off so they could listen to Ian.

Our good friend Joe Aquilina, head of the Full Gospel Business Men, also worked for Maltese TV and had his own Sunday morning programme. Joe extended invitations to both Ian and Noel to sing on TV. Ian was to go out live on Easter Sunday, and he did a fantastic song about Jesus' crucifixion and resurrection. The chorus was, *"Rise He has risen, Rise He is here, death has been conquered, now no reason to fear."* It was amazing. Joe then made a whole programme around Noel, which involved him singing many of his well-known worship songs at different locations on the ship. We were so pleased that these two great servants could be seen and heard by so many, and they certainly blessed us.

Most of what we did, though, was of course less glamorous and took place on the streets. Regular open-air meetings took place, especially in buzzing Valletta. At one such meeting a Swedish lady, Maria, came forward and gave her life to the Lord. The next day she brought her half-Irish, half-Maltese husband, Patrick, to visit us on the ship, where he too gave his life to the Lord. This lovely couple became a blessing to many in Malta and worship leaders in the church. Eventually they set up their own mission and minister to outcasts in the Philippines. Just as Jesus multiplied the loaves and fishes, so too can He multiply our humble efforts. Isn't that so exciting?

The ship, being "neutral," turned out to be a great place for interdenominational meetings. Leaders meetings, prayer meetings, all sorts of events took place on board, even a wedding reception. Having accommodations for fifty-two, it was no problem if people wanted to stay over, and we had many visitors fly out to stay with us. We also had two meeting rooms on board, an extensive library, even a "Charlie," as the secondhand clothes store on OM ships is affectionately known. It was also a great opportunity to meet local people, fishermen, sailors, and tradespeople. Men, in particular, who perhaps wouldn't visit a church would gladly be shown around a ship and even offer to help, which some did. Over the years we made many friends. One of the best friends I have had was Englishman Tony, married to Maltese Mary.

Tony wasn't a churchgoer, though he was a Catholic. He was a bit of a rough diamond but with a heart of gold. I say *was* because sadly Tony is no longer with us, and I will explain more on that in the last chapter. Tony was a mechanic, and over the ten years being based in Malta, we ran several old bangers that often broke down. Tony would come and get us, sort it out, and fix the problem and never take any money for it, or very little anyway. He sometimes helped out with mechanical things on the ship too. We will always be indebted to Tony and Mary.

On a ship at sea, it's important to realise that if there is a fire you can't call the fire brigade, equally you can't call for an ambulance or the police. You don't have mains electricity or gas (obviously), so you really do have to be self-sufficient and thus need people with all sorts of skills or a willingness to learn. I was so grateful to my team for the way they approached the tasks at hand. Whilst some professionals came and went, this "youth" group eventually learnt all the skills necessary. We didn't have the luxury of saying, "You're the navigator, and you're the engineer," etc. We all had to be willing to move out of our comfort zones and learn things we never ever dreamed we would one day be doing. John became an excellent marine engineer, having had some previous experience on the *Logos,* and in the end even Adam and I could start and operate the engines and often did. Everyone learnt to steer the ship, some learnt to navigate, use VHF radio, and chip and paint. It was an interesting time.

Also on a ship you can't send your kids to school, though we did later on when we got into an established pattern and the school our kids went to had a three-month summer holiday, ideal for our summer missions. In the early days, though, it was school on the ship, led by Hilary, for our Sarah and Theo and Willeka's son

Mika and daughter Mirjam. Matt wasn't born at this time. Theo and Willeka were a lovely Dutch couple, and Theo was our first chief engineer. At that time we had a Dutch chef too, a proper one with his own uniform, hat, and set of knives.

The whole adventure of living by faith also continued in Malta. Often when we were without food, some local fisherman would turn up and give us some of his catch. The Christmas turkey one year was provided by local friends—the only thing was it was alive. We bottled out of doing the deadly deed, but Pastor Abe, more experienced in this type of thing, came to the rescue. One of the greatest answers to prayer in the area of provision, though, was when we really were completely out of food and had no money to buy anything. In our group devotions that morning, we brought this need before the Lord. A few hours later, a ship tied up alongside us, as there was no berth space on the quayside. Apparently they were doing an entire crew change. I met the new chief steward/purser. He told me that whenever he joins a new ship, he clears out all the food on board and replenishes it with new stock. He asked if we would like the old stock. "Yes, please," we said, and the rest of the day was spent loading the *Redeemer* with what we estimated was £4000 worth of food and provisions, including steaks and all sorts of food we never would have bought ourselves. Thank You, Lord, that You hear and answer prayer and give us abundantly more than we can ask or think (Ephesians 3:20-21).

The storm that hit Malta shortly after our arrival (briefly referred to in chapter 6) was said by all to be the worst in living memory. Torrential rain turned the quayside into something that looked like Niagara Falls. Storm- to hurricane-force winds were battering everything, and the Gregale was sending its huge swell into the harbour relentlessly, breaking the mooring lines of ship after ship as they rose up and down. The ship we were worried about was not our own but *Big Glory,* the huge 150,000-tonne bulk carrier we were next to. If she broke loose, our little vessel would be flattened like a crisp bag full of air, being squashed. The problem with big ships in confined spaces is that their mooring lines are virtually vertical and so all too easily snap. We spent the night on the bridge or tending to our own moorings, all the time keeping an eye on *Big Glory* and being ready to evacuate if necessary. On the VHF radio, we could hear ships in desperate trouble all over the harbour. Many had broken completely free, and there simply weren't enough tugs to go round. *Big Glory* did break some moorings and looked perilously close to breaking away completely. Before she did, though, a tug appeared and kept her alongside whilst they replaced the ropes.

Eventually the storm passed, and once again we were picking up the pieces, yet praising God for His protection. We hadn't broken a single rope, and ours was the only ship in the harbour that could claim that. However, after our trip down to Malta and now this, I wondered what the team must have thought about it all? Had I led them up the garden path? None of this had been expected, at least not on this scale, and yet we had seen so many answers to prayer. Though tired and exhausted, we could only go forward in faith.

It was about this time too that we faced up to the fact that the Vietnamese boat people problem was over and asked God if there were other things He wanted us to do. After all, we were well situated to reach out to Sicily, Italy, Greece, Turkey, Yugoslavia, Cyprus, and even Albania. So that is what we did.

In fact, we went to all those places, except Albania, which was still communist then and had a minefield offshore. We didn't give up on Albania, though. Instead, we sent in tracts attached to helium balloons from just outside the minefield. (The full story follows in a later chapter.) At the end of each mission, we would return to Malta for the winter and work with the churches there.

We also ministered in a children's home in the former Yugoslavia just two weeks before war broke out there. Many children came to the Lord before being sent back to Sarajevo. We received a phone call from one in the midst of the bombings before the line went dead. We were grateful that though they were going through horrors and terror, they had Jesus with them. (Again, the full story comes later.)

The Lord started to send us people from all over: Germany, Sweden, the USA, and Malta. We were becoming a truly international group. Gill Smith from England joined us and proved to be a major blessing over many years. Others came just for the summer. Claire Bartello from Malta joined us and was instrumental to many of the initiatives we would embark on, including a meeting with the Maltese prime minister. Mauriceo and Shauna LaBorde joined us from Venezuela.

It was time to plan the first mission, and the Lord seemed to be laying Istanbul on our hearts. Istanbul hadn't had a mission ship visit for twenty-five years when the *Logos* was last there. In fact, the Lord was speaking to many about Istanbul. OM was focusing on it that year, and Ichthus in London was sending teams there, as were other groups. It seemed like we were hearing correctly, which was important, as this was not going to be an easy place to go and could be quite dangerous. Turkey officially is a secular country but in reality is very Muslim, and it was and is common for Christians to be murdered.

We wouldn't do this mission in one go but via Sicily and Greece, where we would also hold outreaches and work with local churches. I was fascinated at the time to read in the Bible that when the apostle Paul left Malta for Syracuse in Sicily, it was on a ship that had the twins Castor and Pollux on its figurehead (Acts 28:11). The *Redeemer* was previously named after one of those twins, the *Castor*, and now we too were setting sail for Sicily, for the first of many adventures to come. Once again, we found ourselves praying like Moses, "If your presence does not go with us, do not lead us up from here" (Exod. 33:15).

The Lord clearly was leading us, though, as the testimonies of the following chapters clearly show.

Ian White

Pastors meeting on board

Open-air ministry in Valletta

Reception after Ian White's concert

Preparing for Istanbul. This team was made up of English, American, German, Swedish, Venezuelan and Maltese.

Starting to gather for March for Jesus. The poster with the ship was made by Joyce Baines of St. Mildred's (pictured at the end of the last chapter doing the finishing touches on the jetty at Tower Bridge).

Chapter Eight

SICILY, GREECE, AND TURKEY

"Go therefore and make disciples of all nations."
(Matthew 28:19)

I wish at this point I could quote the apostle Paul, who said in Acts 28:12, *"And landing at Syracuse we stayed there three days."* But I can't, as I bottled the Syracuse bit. You see this was my first voyage as Master, which meant I had to learn to berth the ship and bring it alongside. How does one learn that? Anyway, I decided Syracuse looked a bit tricky and opted for the safer version of nearby Augusta, with its huge, open harbour where we could anchor and go ashore in our RIB. Also we had a contact in Augusta, a local Pentecostal pastor, who had invited us to work along-side his church in mission.

After Sicily we headed for Istanbul. To break the journey, we anchored a couple of times at various

Greek islands. This gave us shelter and a good night's sleep. We even had a couple of runs ashore and after one such visit, a sheepish John and Julie came back aboard and announced their engagement. Julie, our chef, obviously realised that the way to an engineer's heart is through his stomach.

Istanbul we knew would not be a picnic. For a start we couldn't just turn up out of the blue. We would need an agent to act for us locally. The agent is responsible to pick up any bills if the ship does a runner. I can't remember how I found this particular agent. It may have been from OM ships, but we were to become good friends. Ironically, he said to me just before we left, that he was a Muslim and he was desperate for work, so he prayed to Allah. Then he said, "I got a phone call from the *Redeemer*! I prayed to my god, and your god answered." Nice one, Lord.

We were planning to work with the Ichthus church in Istanbul and whilst we had an address and phone numbers, we didn't know where it was. We were looking to moor in the marina but thought we might be too big, so I decided to go to anchor a few miles out from the main city and check the marina out in the morning. It was a Saturday, and we anchored about ten at night. At first light some of us went ashore to make phone calls and check things out. The first building we went into was a hotel, and it turned out that this hotel was where the Ichthus church met, and all our friends were there in the lobby! It was yet another goose-bump moment and a sign the Lord was with us and guiding our steps.

We were too big for the marina, so we decided we would move closer to the centre of the city and remain at anchor, running teams ashore again in the RIB. Our numbers would increase as Ichthus was putting a team on board who had come out from the UK. Many would later say what a blessing it was after a day's outreach in what could be a pretty grim and oppressive environment to get a boat out to a Christian oasis in the middle of the harbour.

From the land our ship looked tiny. I remember looking at it from the grounds of the famous mosque there as the call to prayer went out across the harbour. It was like Goliath looking down on a tiny David, but then I knew how that story ended up!

Other mission ships had used Greek names, which often gave them a bit of cover in situations like this. We had been clear, though, about naming our ship the *Redeemer* (the name above all names, as the song goes). It really didn't give us any cover, though, and nobody was in any doubt about our business.

At one point we had the entire Ichthus group on board for a meal and a prayer meeting. This included families with lots of little children, who all came out in boats and climbed our rope ladder. Most found it exciting; some, I think, terrifying. Just as the group was leaving, we were raided by the so-called secret, or special, police. The women and children who had climbed down into the boat had to stay there, even though there was a huge swell and the boat was being thrown around. Meanwhile the "police" came on and interrogated everybody. Eventually everyone was allowed to leave except Nigel, the leader of the Ichthus church in Istanbul, and a lady named Stephanie. They were told to stay on board; the police would come back for them. However, they managed to flag down a fishing boat and get ashore, much to my relief, as I didn't want to see the church there harmed. It did occur to me, though, that when they returned, they would arrest me instead. Fortunately, they never came back, but I was informed by my agent the next day that we would be fined $2000 and had to leave.

To be honest we were ready to leave by this time. The mission had come to an end, but we obviously weren't too happy about the fine, and for what? I thought of all the people who supported us sacrificially. The giving of our Seacare prayer partners had been an incredibly humbling experience, and yet sadly we had no choice but to pay this if we were to leave.

Also, before we could go, we needed fuel, and they said we couldn't have any! They said we would have to take it at Canakkale in the Dardanelles. I wasn't sure that we could even make Canakkale with the fuel we had. Yet at the same time, I knew we needed to go before they really turned nasty. So we set sail. It had been a good mission, though we clearly had ruffled a few feathers.

As we approached Canakkale, I called them up on the VHF radio. "No, you can't stop here," they said. "Keep going." (We really had ruffled some feathers!) I pointed out that we were out of fuel and our ship would soon stop running and be a hazard to navigation and ourselves. "Keep going" was the reply. This was a very serious situation we were now getting into.

Crazy as it seems, we came up with a plan. The nearest safe haven was Alexandroupolis, just over the border in Greece. There was a very strong current running north to south in the Dardanelles, and we were going south. There was also a very strong wind from the north. The ship had a large sail used primarily to keep her head to the wind in storms. Could this sail be used to harness the northerly wind, and with the current could we still get down the Dardanelles? We thought we would find out. Actually, we didn't have much choice really.

It was amazing. Certainly I think it was the fastest the *Redeemer* has ever sailed. We flew out of the southern end of the Dardanelles. It was completely exhilarating, and somehow we made it all the way to Alexandroupolis.

Having just been through what we had in Turkey, we didn't want to be upsetting the Greek authorities. It had just been in all the news that a YWAM (Youth With A Mission) team had been thrown in jail for proselytising in Athens. However, we linked up with a local church that was more than happy to give us the green light to hold open-air meetings; and so that's what we did, every single night, and they were the best-attended meetings we ever had, often with over a hundred present. Mauriceo from Venezuela and his American wife, Shauna, were in their element with the sketch board, as was Adam with his rope tricks. It turned out to be one of the best places we ever went.

Whilst we had never intended going to Alexandroupolis, one of our team had had a vision similar to the "Macedonian Call" the apostle Paul received, and so here we were now in Macedonia not far from Philippi and the island of Samothrace, clearly visible from Alexandroupolis (Acts 16:11).

The summer was over, and it was time to head back to Malta. On the way I got a phone call from Simon Kreitem, now back running our UK office at London Bridge. "Gale Force 9 to Storm force 10 on its way and a huge swell." Thanks, Simon. We headed for the shelter of a bay on the Greek mainland. It took both anchors down to stop us being driven ashore. The Mediterranean can really catch you out if you're not careful. It had been an eventful summer. Surely next year it couldn't be as exciting and dangerous as this, we thought—or could it?

At anchor off Istanbul, directly opposite the hotel the church met in.

Alexandroupolis, Greece

Outreach in Greece

Chapter Nine

BALLOONS TO ALBANIA

"For the weapons of our warfare are not carnal but mighty in God for the pulling down of strongholds." (2 Corinthians 10:4)

Nobody knew for sure if the minefield was real, but according to the chart, Albania was mined up to twelve miles offshore. It was twelve miles (and a bit) where we now sat quietly, drifting in the dark with our engines off. It was too dangerous to go any nearer and risky enough even being here with patrol boats around and armed smugglers with fast powerboats full of fuel drums to get them to Italy and back. It was going to be a long night.

Down below, our team was filling balloons with helium gas. The plan was to attach tracts, printed in Albanian and sealed in waterproof plastic, and send them into Albania. The tracts also contained the frequency of Trans World Radio's Albanian broadcasts. Simon had spent most of the year researching how to do this. Too much helium would take the balloons too high, and they would burst. Too little and they would come down in the sea before reaching land. Special balloons were purchased, and we had to load several huge, six-foot-tall metal gas bottles of helium in Malta before we left. Adam Charon even invented a device for tying the knots in the balloons that saved everyone from having to use their fingers. Of course we needed the wind to blow from the right direction, and tonight it was. The conditions were perfect.

Nerves were a little fraught and not helped by the fact that every now and then a balloon would burst, making a bang not totally unlike gunfire. I stayed on the bridge to regularly check our position in case we drifted towards the minefield and to keep a look out of course. The engines, though stopped, were on standby in case we had to move quickly.

By now our family had grown with the arrival of Matt. Sarah was now nearly five, and Matt as a newborn baby was finding his sea legs. Matt had been born in Malta at the hospital in Msida, with the help of a no-nonsense midwife.

I remember her saying to Hilary, *"Sorry, no gas. It wasn't delivered today. Do as I say, and you will be fine!"* And she was. In fact, mother and baby were home eight hours later. In biblical times it was traditional to dedicate babies to the Lord eight days after they were born. Matt, like Sarah, was born on Saturday, so it was easy to do just that the following Sunday morning in our church, with Pastor Joe Fenech-Laudi doing the honours.

As I write this, I have thought, "Was I crazy and/or selfish to put my family into this situation?" Here they all were sitting on the edge of a minefield, and goodness knows what would happen if an Albanian patrol boat found us. I can only conclude that God had clearly spoken to us about this project. He had provided every-thing needed without our asking anyone for anything. I knew we were in the centre of His will for us, and there is no better or safer place to be. We had His peace, though we needed to be careful as well, and this was about as close to the wind as I ever wanted to sail.

As the balloons were released in the night sky and blown towards Albania, we decided to pray over the whole project and to intercede for the nation. We were led very much to pray along the lines of the apostle Paul in his second letter to the Corinthians when he said, "*Our weapons of warfare are not carnal but mighty in God for the pulling down of strongholds and every pretence that sets its mind against God.*"

At that time Albania was one of the last communist strongholds with an atheist philosophy that declared that God was dead, so it seemed an appropriate way to pray. There were, of course, Christians in the country working away, and there was a Catholic church. The government, however, was atheistic and ruled the country with an iron fist.

By about 3:00 a.m. we decided we had better move on. We hadn't let all our five thousand balloons off, but we figured we could let the remainder off from a position near Corfu later in the voyage if we got the right wind direction. We had taken a bit longer than we anticipated, and we knew there must be some nervy Albanian military looking at a radar screen somewhere and questioning why this apparently broken-down vessel, so close to their waters was taking so long to fix its engines and get moving. Also, some of the first balloons we released would have reached land by now and we could be in big trouble. So we set sail for the two ports of call we had decided to visit in Yugoslavia. What happened next gives me goose bumps to this day.

We were a few hours into our voyage, and I was still on the bridge. I had tuned our MF Sailor Radio (which allows us to send a Mayday if in trouble) to the BBC World Service. The news was on: *"Breaking News. All over Tirana, the capital of Albania, people are running into foreign embassies and claiming asylum."* I don't think I had ever heard anything about Albania in the news ever. It was a communist stronghold, and nothing ever changed in Albania. That night it did. It was the beginning of the collapse of communism. It started on a night when a bunch of youngsters sent the Word of God into that nation and prayed for the tearing down of strongholds. I don't know if that was a coincidence. I can't wait to ask God about it, though.

We had no idea that Yugoslavia was about to become breaking news too. Our pictures of Yugoslavia were gained from holiday brochures that showed nice beaches and friendly people. But this too was another communist country about to implode. We had no idea we were only weeks away from a war that would shock the world with its ethnic cleansing and atrocities not seen since World War II.

The highlight for us was a place called Cavtat, near Dubrovnik. You have to sail through a tiny narrow entrance, and then it opens up into a beautiful circular bay. We could have been, quite possibly the biggest ship they had ever seen in there. There was no way we could berth alongside anywhere, so we anchored in the middle of the bay and used our inflatable RIB to get ashore.

At this point, and not for the first time, we seemed to be out of money. As we came together as a team, we felt the Lord was calling us to go ahead in faith and trust Him. After all, He had never let us down before, and we had seen so many miraculous examples of His provision. The deal was that we would send two teams ashore and they would stay ashore, live there, be directed by God what to do, and rely on Him for provision. I felt a bit guilty about this because I again would have to stay with the ship and make sure the anchor didn't drag. Everyone was up for it, though, and there was a real sense of excitement about it. As it happened, it turned out to be one of the most amazing experiences everyone involved had ever had. I didn't need to feel guilty about staying on the ship; I was the one who missed out!

The two teams headed off in different directions. One team decided to stay in the main town and reach out in whatever way they could. They ended up late at night singing in the open-air bars and restaurants. However, they were singing Christian worship songs. I will never forget hearing "Majesty," which I could hear on the bridge of the ship in the middle of the harbour. It sounded wonderful, and the diners and holidaymakers loved it, as did the owners of the restaurants who gave them free meals at the end of the evening before they returned to their camping in the woods. People gave them money too, without them asking for it. They did all sorts of practical tasks during the day and really blessed the community.

The second team was led to work in a children's home. These disaffected children from Sarajevo were there to get some respite from bad health and difficult situations at home. The team was allowed to take services there; and to put it in a nutshell, it was as if revival broke out amongst the kids. They were worshipping and having visions and prophecies; it was incredible. What we didn't know, though, was that we were just two weeks away from war, and these kids would be returned to Sarajevo, perhaps the worst place they could be, as it was about to become hell on earth. It was great, though, that these kids would at least not have to go through that alone. They now knew Jesus and God the Father. They could pray; and if the worst happened, they would be in a better place. I will never forget some time later back in Malta, Claire, one of the leaders of that team, getting a phone call from one of the little boys in that group. He was back in Sarajevo, the war was waging, and he seemed OK before the phone went dead. We continue to pray for those kids, wherever they are today.

After Cavtat we went to Srebreno, a little closer to Dubrovnik and where most people managed an excursion into the capital. Again we anchored off. Our time here, though, was cut short by a dangerous forest fire. Huge, beautiful forested mountains formed the backdrop of Srebreno, but they often gave rise to katabatic winds, the dread of many a sailor. Warm air rises up the mountain, where it is cooled and becomes heavier and denser. Then, like a tonne weight, it drops back down the mountain and creates winds of storm force 10 that can travel twenty miles out to sea. We were about to experience what happens when the mountainside is on fire and a katabatic wind starts.

Unfortunately, most of the crew were ashore when the fire started. What seemed like a small fire initially was soon a raging inferno racing down the mountain on the back of storm-force katabatic winds. I was concerned for the safety of my team and crew. If I am honest, I may have panicked a little bit; but from where I stood on the ship, this looked mega serious.

Adam started running the inflatable ashore to rescue our team who were by now heading back towards the quayside. It was more the smoke that concerned me, as this was way ahead of the fire. Eventually everyone was accounted for and back on board. Then we heard a Mayday on the radio. Somebody else was in trouble; and before we knew it, Adam was off on a rescue mission.

My concern was that the wind was so strong that it could get under the bow of the boat as Adam rode the waves and flip it over backwards. But Adam had become the master of handling the RIB, which was amazing, as he's from Minnesota and had never even seen the sea before he joined Seacare. Now he was out rescuing people in winds gusting to force 10. As it happened, this turned out to be a false alarm, and fortunately Adam made it back safe and sound.

It was time to head back to Malta for the winter programme, stopping off at Corfu to hopefully send the remaining balloons to Albania. The excitement, however, wasn't over yet. It should have been a straightforward trip back, but we had heard by now that communism in Albania really had collapsed and that refugees were fleeing in boats. Were we yet to rescue some boat people, the original purpose of the whole project?

111

So we hung around again off the coast of Albania for a while, but it wasn't to be. We didn't find any boat people, so we continued on to Corfu, where we did release the rest of the balloons.

Sadly in Corfu Janice Chard phoned me with news that John's dad had been taken ill. Reg was a great guy. He came out to the ship in Holland when we bought it and did all sorts of jobs around the ship. His wife, Ellen, and their daughter, Katie, came out to Malta when we first arrived and organised our Sarah's third birthday party. I literally ran to the airport and got tickets for John and Julie for the first flight back to the UK. John was in time to see his dad and have a very special and precious time with him before the end. It was with great sadness that we sailed on to Malta.

When we rounded the boot of Italy we decided we would take a break and anchor overnight in the Bay of Taranto. It would give us a good night's sleep before the last leg to Malta.

All was well, but we hadn't realised how agitated the Italian military was getting about their new problem—the Albanian boat people. They were looking for suspicious vessels. Our ship was also very old. It had a gun place-ment on the foredeck, a relic from the Second World War, and a very strange looking direction finder aerial. Some might think we were a spy ship. Needless to say, our night wasn't so peaceful after all.

We were just settling down for the night when a Guardia De Financia (Italian) patrol boat started heading towards us at high speed. Before we knew it, they were alongside and jumping aboard. They wore military uniforms and were armed with machine guns and pistols. The worst of it was that Hilary was down in a below-decks cabin putting Sarah and Matthew to bed and reading them a bedtime story, when they burst in on her in a very aggressive way. (Perhaps one bedtime story the kids won't forget.) They searched the cabin and the entire ship, looking for whatever. When they realised we were not doing anything wrong, they became very friendly and left peacefully.

We couldn't wait to get back to Malta, the country that had seemed to adopt us and was rapidly becoming home. Sailing into Grand Harbour, Valletta is always an amazing experience. Even today if I go to Malta, I go by sea from Italy so that I can experience it again. We were safely "home" after an incredibly exciting, if a little dangerous, time. The only down side was turning on the TV and seeing the places we had just been to now being bombed and shelled. This certainly had been a frontline mission. "Lord, look after those kids. Thank You for allowing us to be part of Your plans." It was awesome.

The kids from Sarajevo in Cavtat

Chapter Ten

INTO THE DARKNESS

*"Shall we indeed accept goodness from our God
and not accept adversity?"* (Job 2:10)

It had been great to see what God had done on these
various missions, and more was yet to come. I felt that
all those who believed in us and supported us would
see that though we didn't do what we had originally
planned, great things still had happened; and hopefully
they were pleased, even proud to be part of it. But what
of the future?

Some of the original team, only teenagers when we
started, were now older, back in the UK, married and
having kids themselves. Things were changing. It was
difficult for me being the master of the ship; I was so
involved that maybe I couldn't see the wood for the
trees.Some of us had different ideas concerning the
way forward. We decided that after the next missions,

we would try to find somewhere to safely lay up the ship and take the entire team back to England for a sabbatical and to do a speaking tour. The next couple of years, though, were to be the toughest we had ever known.

The next summer saw us in Cyprus and Crete, before laying up for the winter. The summer after that was "deliverance" from the nightmare of the problems our lay-up brought us with time in the beautiful towns of Navplion and Tolo on the Greek mainland, before returning to Malta.

We arrived at the anchorage off Limassol, Cyprus, at the same time the first Gulf War broke out. The Suez Canal had been closed, and hundreds of ships had been diverted to the Limassol anchorage. Ironically, we anchored between two ships called *Mohammed 1* and *Mohammed 2*. We, of course, were the *Redeemer*! We were also next to the RAF base at Akrotiri and listened to reports on the news of Saddam Hussein's intentions to fire Scud missiles at the base. How did we always end up where things were happening? We knew, though, that even if it was front line again, we were where God wanted us, and so it wasn't going to be an issue.

Ichthus, the church in London we were linked with, had sent teams out to Cyprus this year to join up with a church plant and training course set up by Ray Mayhew and presently being run by Steve Critchlow. So once again we worked with Ichthus and another local Pentecostal church we had links with. We didn't know then, but in the years to come we would lead an Ichthus congregation in Southeast London that would have several people in it whom we met in Cyprus and Istanbul.

We had an amazing time in Cyprus, which felt more like the Middle East than the Mediterranean, perhaps because so many Arabs were stranded there. Everyone was so open and friendly and interested to talk and open to the gospel. We were sorry when our time there came to an end, not least because they make the most amazing souvlakis (like a kebab) and sell them so cheaply.

The next stop was Crete, the most southern part of Europe. Once again we were following in the footsteps of St. Paul, who strongly advised the master and owners of the ship he was on to stay there for the winter, only to be overruled (Acts 27). However, it was the providence of God that he would eventually be shipwrecked on Malta. Fortunately for us, we didn't have to follow him literally, though we did come close a couple of times off Malta. It was good to have Simon and Janice Kreitem back with us in Cyprus and now for the voyage to Crete.

We linked up with a great Pentecostal church in Iraklion and again had an amazing time and didn't want to leave. In fact, we weren't sure we could leave, as there was a national strike and we couldn't access money from the bank. Worse than that, though, was that rubbish hadn't been collected for weeks and there were rats everywhere. We didn't know then that this was only the beginning of our problem with rats.

We had enough fuel to get us to the next port, Elefsina near Athens, where we would lay up, but we had no provisions. We decided to leave as scheduled. Just before we slipped our moorings, several cars and a van came down the quayside sounding their horns. It was our friends from the church coming to see us off and present us with boxes and boxes of food and provisions. They even had a massive pack of luxury nappies/diapers, which Hilary, who had been using towel ones on baby Matt, had been praying for specifically. We can be specific with our God; He cares, and so did the wonderful believers in Iraklion. Whether we are praying for tens of thousands of pounds to fill up with fuel or go into dry dock, or praying for nappies for Matt or a play park for Sarah, it all matters to God; and we can believe Him for answers.

Elefsina, near Piraeus, Athens, was supposed to be very safe, as it is completely landlocked. Dauntingly, it was known as the "graveyard" for ships before they are scrapped. On the plus side, Youth With A Mission bought their ship the *Anastasis* there. (*Anastasis* is Greek for resurrection—very appropriate in a graveyard.)

Elefsina was to become a nightmare for us, and to this day I don't know if we heard God wrong or if I got it wrong. I just don't know. I had spent so many hours researching for a safe lay-up place, and this seemed to be it; but things were about to go terribly wrong.

It all started off well, though we had moved into a different world. Like in Istanbul we were forced to take an agent, and here too we needed a pilot to guide us into the harbour. Both were very expensive.

On the plus side, we made friends with a great guy, a New Zealander named Wayne Ritchie, who ran a church in Piraeus. He used to preach on the trains, and Adam joined him sometimes. He had many Africans in his church who liked to dance, and we often finished the service doing the conga around the outside of the room.

We appointed a watchman to look after the ship, now tied up between several rusty, old Russian hulks made of iron, so that we could return to the UK. We thought the ship would be safe here, but we were wrong.

Amazingly, back in England we were offered free accommodation in a house belonging to a Brethren Church in Romford, Essex. This became our base for several months, and just down the road was an evangelical Christian school that Sarah joined. It was all perfect.

Our speaking tour took us all over the country, and we were able to share all that God had done, along with our vision. One special place we went was Nailsea, near Bristol. This is where we met John Luft, a local pastor and soon to become a precious friend. John wanted to help us in any way he could, and he and his wife, Jane, offered to run our office if we relocated it to Nailsea. We had been struggling to man our London Bridge office, so this was ideal. Better still, it came with a congregation willing to visit us regularly in Malta and send our newsletters out. What wonderful provision. John also introduced me to many of the Christian Leaders in the Bristol area, like Rob Scott-Cooke, and we even met in George Muller's old place. John once sat in George Muller's old chair so forcefully that it went "crack," but fortunately it stayed intact. I thought it was a nice touch because George Muller's story was a major inspiration to me when I was starting the Seacare project.

We appointed John the UK Director of Seacare, and he became a trustee. He and Jane and their congregation were such a blessing to us. They had real servant hearts, putting out our newsletters and regularly flying out to see us. John showed me the best model of accountability I had seen, not just expecting me to be accountable "to" him and the trustees, but also choosing himself to be proactive and accountable "for" me. He asked the hard, often-uncomfortable questions, but it made us feel safe and cared for. If ever I needed him, he would be on the next plane—amazing.

Back in Romford we received a telephone call from our agent in Greece. There had been a big storm, and the *Redeemer* was severely damaged! How can this be? we wondered. It's a totally sheltered harbour, and there was a watchman who could have put more fenders out. We soon realised, of course, that there was no such watchman. Apparently, there was a dent down the port side of the vessel forty feet long and six feet high and at least a foot deep. It was above the waterline, so there was no danger of sinking, but it was not very pretty. It was two days before Christmas. What should we do?

I had been hoping to have a traditional family Christmas with Hilary, Sarah, and Matt. It was even snowing. Adam Charon, bless him, offered to fly out on his own and assess the situation. Adam is such a loyal and faithful person with such a servant heart, and people like that are easy to take for granted. Years later, I found myself writing to Adam and apologising for, at times, doing just that. Gill Smith too was like that. Our team, though small, was comprised of some very special people.

Adam confirmed the worst, and we felt that we probably should go back ourselves. There wasn't much we could do, but we didn't want to leave Adam there on his own. Now we had another mission—to get the ship out of that dark and depressing place. But that was something easier said than done.

In the end we decided not to rush back because Wayne Ritchie had offered Adam accommodation in Piraeus, so he was in good hands and enjoying being in fellowship and helping with the church's outreach. They in turn helped him. One man collected some old lorry tyres and took them and Adam down to Elefsina so that we could have extra fenders on the ship.

The agents were demanding more money, and we were still expected to pay for the watchman who wasn't watching. It was like being a fly trapped in a spider's web. How would we ever get out of this place?

The first ones to join Adam back at the ship were Gill and her friend, my friend Rick with whom I had trained as a navigating officer back at college, and our dear friend Captain Denys Collins, who returned once again. I then joined them, followed by Hilary and the kids and Clare Bartello.

When we got back to the ship, we found it had some new inhabitants—rats! Little Sarah said to Mum Hilary, "A big shoe has just run past the galley." It wasn't a shoe but a giant rat! It was going to take us weeks to get rid of these rats because the ships we were tied up to were infested with them. Adam and I lightened the situation a bit. We started tying furry puppets on string to the inside of door handles, so that when you opened a door the "rat" flew out at you. Sick I know, but we were desperate. It was laugh or cry. Adam made it his personal mission to rid us of these rats and was constantly devising elaborate and imaginative "traps."

We had no monies coming in either, and I had serious back trouble and a mega bout of food poisoning. Times were really grim and tough. We used to worry that a rat would bite our kids whilst they slept. The damage to the side of the ship would cost at least £50,000 to repair, and we couldn't pay the agent or the port fees, take on fuel and water, or even buy food.

Each day, though I was in agony with my back, I would climb down the rope ladder and take the shuttle boat ashore. This was followed by a forty-five-minute rickety bus ride to Piraeus that shook my aching spine to the core. I would meet the agent and seek justice regarding all the bills they were throwing at us. Why should we pay for a watchman who wasn't there? Then I would go to the cash point to try to get some money out for provisions. Invariably, day after day it would say, "You have insufficient funds." One day I took our daughter Sarah with me, and we had funds! I could take £50 out. I treated Sarah to a snack on the way back. Fortunately, she didn't eat the same thing I did, for when we got back to Elefsina, I was writhing in agony, and my body violently rejected and ejected every ounce of food and liquid in me. It was awful and embarrassing, and I still had to get little Sarah safely back to the ship on the water taxi. Miraculously, I somehow managed it. I remember thinking, "This really is the pits," and somehow I knew we had to get out of this place and that we all needed to do some serious praying. It appeared that we were no longer enjoying the blessings we had become used to. Was the *Redeemer,* like the many other ships in Elefsina, "the graveyard," going to spend the rest of her days here as just another rotting hulk? Were we doing something wrong? Was it just an attack? There could be any number of reasons. In the Bible we read that Job, who suffered so much, had to remind his wife to trust God in the bad times too, saying, *"Shall we indeed accept goodness from our God and not adversity?"* (Job 2:10).

As we were reunited again as a team and met daily to pray, things started to slowly but surely improve. Our goal was simple: get out of Elefsina. We weren't looking beyond that. Funds started to come in again, and an engineer named Jochen joined us from Germany. We started in faith to prepare the ship for sea. After about a month, we were ready. We had agreed to a compromise with the agents regarding the fees. We took on a bit of fuel and some provisions and ordered our pilot. It took several hours of complicated anchor work to free ourselves from the Russian hulks, but soon the beautiful sound of our engines could be heard once again. We were in the narrow channel out of Elefsis Bay, heading towards Piraeus and freedom. Once we dropped the pilot off, we had to navigate the tricky waters around Piraeus with what seemed like hundreds of kamikaze ferries darting in and out. We were back from the dead, and we were free!

We headed for the small island of Idhra, just forty miles southwest of Athens, where we would anchor, celebrate our escape, and enjoy a much-needed good night's sleep.

After Idhra we sailed on to the beautiful towns of Navplion and Tolo on the Greek mainland. There was nowhere to go alongside in Tolo, so once again we anchored, but this time in water so incredibly deep that I was concerned that our windlass would struggle to bring the anchor back up. The nearby town of Navplion, after inspection, had plenty of quayside and was very sheltered, so we decided to move there. Fortunately, the anchor came up without a problem, if a little slowly.

In Navplion we met a German believer named Ute. She was thrilled that we had come. We provided her with much-needed fellowship, and we even had a German crewman. We sought to minister as much as we could in these places, but this time we didn't have our huge summer teams. We came across a large camp of Romany travellers on the outskirts of Navplion and visited them regularly.

We were convinced that the events of the last year had brought to an end a particular phase of ministry and was heralding in another. If we hadn't have laid the ship up, we never would have met many of the people back in the UK who would go on to play a significant part in the future, but equally the ship wouldn't have been damaged and we would have been spared a pretty tough time. It was hard to understand it all. One thing was clear to us all, though: it was time to return "home."

I took out the navigation charts and plotted a course to Malta. I have been privileged to sail into three of the most beautiful harbours in the world; Rio de Janeiro, Hong Kong, and Valletta. I just loved sailing back into

Grand Harbour, Valletta, after each summer mission. This time we had been away well over two years, and it had never felt so good.

Berthed again in Vittoriosa, the locals were pleased to see us, and I knew Hilary and Sarah would soon be resuming their early morning ritual of heading into the backstreets to the bakers for fresh Maltese bread. Fellowship with our friends and the churches was renewed, and life seemed good again. Of course, we were still battered and bruised, and I recalled a message I had heard from Dr. Alan Redpath about soldiers not accomplishing much if they never got blood on their tunics. We would definitely need a short time of recovery and a time of listening to God about the future. We were like Jonah being spewed out of the fish's belly. We had been rescued, the *Redeemer* had risen from the grave, but we were still a bit shaken up and still had as many questions as answers.

Chapter Eleven

MALTA AGAIN

"And the natives showed us unusual kindness, for they kindled a fire and made us all welcome because of the rain ... they also honored us in many ways and when we departed they provided such things as were necessary." (Acts 28:2, 10)

So here we were back in Malta, safely "home"; and it was wonderful. The locals were pleased to see us, and the churches were too. We would put our kids in local schools, where they had three months holiday every summer—plenty of time for our missions. Elefsina and the rats were a thing of the past, and things were looking up.

The next years would see us working more in and around Malta. The Pickering family from England would join us, along with the Von Medings from Chicago, among others. Both these families, as well as being totally committed to outreach with Seacare, would also throw their lot in with local churches of their choice and be a real help and blessing there.

Recently a Maltese pastor told me that he was writing a book about the history of the church in Malta and would be including our ship the *Redeemer* because, in his words, we had played a significant part in it. I was humbled by this and tried to reflect on what we had done. I knew we had done a lot of outreach and seen people come to the Lord. One couple who came to the Lord have now started their own mission in the Philippines. But what else? I was also only too aware that I had made plenty of mistakes.

The church situation in Malta was a political mine-field when we arrived. We were mindful of how much damage short-term people who don't understand the history can do, and we certainly didn't want to do that. We trod very carefully.

Malta was a Catholic country, more "Rome" than Rome itself. As evangelicals this was interesting. Hilary, pregnant with Matt and not feeling too well, had visited a doctor in one Mediterranean country who immediately had offered to perform an abortion. We had been really shocked by this. Thankfully, that wouldn't happen in Malta. It felt good to be in a Christian country, even if our doctrines were different.

Several evangelical churches had been planted in Malta and had their roots in places as far afield as

Scandinavia, the USA, Africa, etc. Each of these new churches had incorporated the theology of the mother churches and the sending missionaries.

Over the years many Catholics converted to this evangelical theology and left the Catholic Church, often facing persecution and ridicule as a result.

For us arriving into this situation alone wouldn't have been a problem. We were evangelicals, and that was that. However, there had been a charismatic renewal amongst a section of the Catholic Church. To all intents and purposes these were genuine, born-again and Spirit-filled believers, who for some reason felt they should stay in the Catholic Church. This, of course, caused a lot of pain to those who had left the Catholic Church and been persecuted for their decision.

This was the situation we confronted, and so we decided to try to be a bridge. Bridges, however, can be lonely places. They just stand there and take every-thing—the wind, the rain, the sleet, and the snow—whilst people walk all over them. At times it felt like that, but we did it anyway, hoping people from different sides would eventually meet each other.

We also figured if we tried to tell these Catholic charismatics that they had to come out of the Catholic Church, we would be doing the very thing we think they have got wrong. We would be playing priest, vicar, and pope and not allowing them to hear from God for themselves. Either we believe in the priesthood of all believers, or we don't. The word *vicar* comes from the word *vicarious;* it means trying to live our spiritual lives through another. Because we believe everyone can go directly to God for him/herself, we can't complain when others choose to do something we don't understand.

We tried to encourage unity. Let's agree to disagree but respect and love one another was our message. We might not understand and maybe never will this side of heaven, but let's love our brothers and sisters in Christ. Not everyone agreed with us, but I think that most respected what we were trying to do. Sometimes these matters are a case of timing. Coming in from outside gave us a different perspective, and hopefully we were of some help and operated with humility, grace, and respect. I am sure we got things wrong at times, but our hearts were in the right place, and experience had shown how important that was to God.

We had to work through all of this on board ship, too, of course. We were from different denominations but also different countries and cultures. We were all Christians, but the Americans didn't drink or smoke, whereas the Dutch and Germans might do both! For the Dutch, Sunday lunch was sandwiches and soup; for the British it was a full roast. A lot of the problems were not theological but cultural and down to people's individual insecurities. We needed to learn about grace.

So we continued to allow the ship to be used for all kinds of cross-denominational meetings—evangelical, charismatic, Full Gospel Business Men, whatever. We were neutral ground and wanted to make the most of that and be as inclusive as possible.

In the middle of all this, of course, we were still a ship and faced all the hazards that went with that, including coming perilously close to being shipwrecked like the apostle Paul. It shouldn't have happened because it was summer, but we were about to lose our engines and be at the mercy of a freak summer storm.

We had sailed up to Paradise Bay on the Northwest corner of the Island. It was one of the few places where we could tie up outside of Valletta, and it meant we could take bunkers and stores, easily go ashore ourselves, and have visitors on board. Although the bay was open and exposed to the west, it was summer and shouldn't be a problem. I also had berthed stern first with an anchor down so that if a swell picked up, I could pull her off the berth a bit so there wouldn't be any damage. However, two things happened that we couldn't have foreseen, and the consequences for us were nearly disastrous.

A metal rod that was part of the equipment needed to start our engines had snapped, and a new one would have to be made before we could sail again. My friend Tony came and took it to an engineering firm that could do it. They said it would take four days. At the same time I noticed a bit of swell was rolling into the bay from the west, which was most unusual for this time of year.

I went to check the weather forecast, and it didn't make good reading. The weather was expected to deteriorate and the wind, sea and swell would continue to increase from the west. We couldn't wait four days for the part, if the seas picked up too much, we would have to sail out. The company said they would do it quicker but couldn't promise. The seas continued to pick up.

I soon realised we had a serious problem, and I decided to evacuate our kids who went and stayed with a family from our church in Paola. Adam Pickering, John and Bernadette's teenage son, became the hero of the day. As the seas increased, we knew that if we didn't put out some really long mooring ropes then the short ones we had would snap and we would break loose. Adam volunteered to do this, despite the fact that the sea and waves were now breaking over the quayside and dock itself.

It had now been three days, and our ship was being lifted up and dropped down again so much that it was no longer a matter of *if* we broke lose but *when,* and when we did, we would probably be lifted up and thrown through the side of the Paradise Bay Hotel next door. We needed that part, but I couldn't leave the ship, so once again it was down to our mechanic friend Tony, who chased it up and brought it out to us. There was no time to lose, Jochen, our German engineer, started to fit it. By now the seas were huge. It was like December, not July. The Gozo ferry had stopped running, and we were in a big storm. I got John to start heaving the anchor, which pulled us away from the quay that we were now smashing into; and all the time Jochen was trying to fit the part. Our RIB was in the water too and being smashed up. Finally, the part was fitted, the anchor was up, and the engines were started, and we sailed away, albeit leaving behind some broken mooring lines and with a damaged RIB. We were all safe, though. Thank You, Lord. That was close. We really hadn't wanted to follow that much in the footsteps of Paul and really be shipwrecked, but we had come very close, far too close.

It was time to think again about the future and hear from God. Jochen was due to return to Germany, and then we wouldn't have an engineer at all; yet the harbour master, rightfully so, could and regularly would expect us to move the ship from berth to berth with very little notice. Why couldn't we ever find an engineer who was free to commit long-term? Was there somebody who was called but not obeying that call? Even so, God was God and had the whole world to choose from. At the start of the project, I had always used that quote: *"God's work done God's way will not lack God's supply."* I couldn't conveniently ignore that principle now, and so I concluded that it was time to either sell the ship or give it to another ministry in a better position to use it. This, of course, was a heartbreaking decision and something we had not really anticipated. Also, it would prove to be something easier said than done and would take some time to achieve. If only we could get it back to England, but before we could contemplate a voyage like that, we knew the classification society would insist on another dry dock; and where would we find the tens of thousands of pounds that would cost or the crew we would need for a two-thousand-mile voyage? We were about to find out.

Chapter Twelve

DRY DOCK AND FAREWELL, MALTA

"Has He said and will He not do it? Or has
He spoken and will He not make it good?"
(Numbers 23:19)

Simon and Janice and John and Julie had long left
Seacare now and were running their own very
successful companies in the UK. However, when they
heard that I wanted to sail the ship back, they knew I
would need some help, and Simon and John decided
to come back and help with the voyage. This was an
amazing turn of events. I counted these guys as my
best friends, and I had deeply missed them and was
touched by their willingness to do this, especially as
Simon in particular had suffered really badly with seasickness on the voyage out. Having John in the engine

room again was a real godsend. The Lord was moving; that was for sure.

The quote for the dry dock was £37,000, a fortune for us, especially in those days. Knowing God was at work, though, fills you with faith and confidence, and we went ahead and booked it. Even more amazing was that Johannes Thomson, chief engineer and marine superintendent with OM ships volunteered to come out and supervise the dry dock. I have memories of Johannes working virtually around the clock for two to three weeks whilst the repairs, surveys, and inspections took place. Just as Mike Poyner from OM Ships had helped us at the start, so here was his colleague Johannes, who we had sailed with on the *Logos,* helping us now. It felt like God was wrapping His arms around us and giving us a big hug.

All the time the Pickerings and Von Medings continued with outreach and serving the local church. John used to do an act in the open air that involved standing perfectly still like a statue, similar to the type of thing you see in Covent Garden in London. Bernadette was very much into music and dance, and Kathy Von Meding was full of energy for evangelism. All their kids were great and a valued part of our crew. The last weeks in Malta were very special. Perhaps nothing was more special than when all the evangelical churches had a joint outreach to Gozo that finished with an amazing time of worship on the Gozo ferry.

YWAM sent us some Discipleship Training Students (DTS) who were largely made up of people from the Middle East. We came particularly close to a couple of Egyptians, one of whom married a Swiss YWAMer. They had their reception party on our ship. Great days.

With the dry dock over and the ship back in the water now, there was just the problem of that bill. Our policy throughout had been not to fund-raise but to make our needs known to God alone through prayer, so that is what we did. We had no problem with organisations that didn't do this; we simply did it because we had been led to and it provided me the security of not being able to proceed unless God was in it. The peace of mind that gave me when putting to sea, always potentially hazardous, with largely untrained volunteers, including my own family, was priceless. The initial excitement of buying the ship ten years earlier had gone, but we still had about fifteen hundred prayer partners and a faithful God. A verse in Scripture I had held onto many times was Numbers 23:19: *"Has He said and will He not do it, has He spoken and will He not make it good?"* It was time to stand on that promise again.

Sure enough the Lord prompted people all over the world to give. To be fair, they knew we had dry-docked. It had been in our newsletter, so they would realise there would be major costs; but we never said what they were or asked anyone to give. It was an exciting way to live, though pretty nerve-racking and testing at times. The answers to prayer we saw, though, were amazing, and they are really the reason I am writing this book: to remind the hundreds who were involved over the years and hopefully to inspire new people who have just now heard of the project by reading the account of it in these pages.

Once again we were able to testify to the faithfulness of a great God and the generosity of our prayer partners as the dry-dock bill was duly paid, freeing the *Redeemer* to sail back to the UK after being "based" in Malta for nine whole years. The crew started to assemble. There was also the other small matter of the £20,000 needed to fill the fuel tanks. We were not there yet. Amazingly, that came in too.

The ship had been such a part of the scenery in Malta that I don't think the reality that we were actually going had sunk in. Malta had become our home. Our son was born there, and we loved the place. I remember feeling more anxious about leaving there than I ever did when we first set sail from the UK into the unknown.

Our eleven-year-old daughter, Sarah, was really looking forward to going back to England and decided for herself that her job on the way back would be to wait on tables. Seven-year-old Matt was leaving the country of his birth for a strange and foreign place called England. They both had been schooled at the international school, where the average class size was about twelve and where they had mixed with the sons and daughters of ambassadors. Soon they would be in an inner city London comprehensive and primary school respectively. No wonder we were anxious!

I remember the few who had been concerned for Sarah's welfare when we sailed away from London and she was just a baby. Looking back, though, I can honestly say that the ship experience was amazing for both her and Matt. It did, however, mark them out as a bit unusual. I remember Sarah getting disciplined at school when the teacher had asked the children to draw a picture of their home and Sarah drew a ship. The teacher hadn't known and just thought she was being naughty. Another time she met a girl on the beach who asked her, "Where do you live?" "I live on a ship," Sarah replied. The girl thought for a moment and then said, "Mmm, well, I live on a helicopter!"

John was joined in the engine room by another German engineer, and my friend Rick, an ex-merchant navy navigating officer, joined us once again. We still had the very experienced Alistair Sutherland, also a qualified Captain. I felt very safe and confident about the voyage that lay before us. It was summer, so the weather should be much better than the voyage out, though we hadn't forgotten the summer storm in Paradise Bay. The voyage would take us along the coasts of Tunisia, Algeria, southern Spain, and then out into the Atlantic Ocean and our dreaded friend, the Bay of Biscay, across the widest part of the channel, and into our destination port of Falmouth, England.

We were finally ready to sail. We had used our cranes to lift our car on board, along with a tiny, pretty Maltese fishing boat we were taking home as a souvenir. We had determined to sail the moment we were ready, as many of the crew had jobs to return to. This meant we couldn't give people a "time," so the send-off was relatively modest, consisting of only those who had heard by word of mouth. We were going to miss these wonderful Maltese believers, people like Franz and Margaret, who were on the quayside now, and the locals who had shown us so much kindness and generosity, amazingly the same experience as that of the apostle Paul two thousand years earlier.

For the last time the *Redeemer* slipped her moorings and sailed out of one of the most amazing harbours in the world. Passing the breakwater, we turned left and headed for the crystal clear waters of Comino and Gozo, which had so impressed us nearly a decade ago when we arrived.

I regretted not getting to see and say good-bye to my great friend Tony, the mechanic who had got us out of so many tough situations, not least the Paradise Bay incident. As I said before, Tony didn't attend church and was a really rough diamond but with a heart of gold. Mary was from the "Three Cities," where our ship was berthed, and they were friends with many of the local people, many of whom were tough guys we had sought to reach out to over the years. I would miss Tony and Mary very much.

A few miles into our journey, however, the VHF radio crackled, "*Redeemer, Redeemer. Come in, Redeemer.*" It was Tony. He apparently owned a handheld VHF set and was now on the coast at St. Paul's Bay watching us. We shared a bit of banter and wished each other well. We had got to say our good-byes!

I didn't know it then, but my relationship with Tony and Mary was far from over and about to intensify dramatically, sadly in tragic circumstances.

Chapter Thirteen

PRESTON, ENGLAND

"So he left the Temple in peace, having embraced his salvation." (Luke 2:29-30)

The voyage back bore no resemblance to the trip out. The sun shone, and the sea was calm. We enjoyed a barbecue on deck and marvelled at the dolphins that gracefully posed and showed off their skills on our bow wave. Sure enough, Sarah waited on tables, and Matt did some chipping and painting. The engines and all the equipment worked beautifully. The thing I remember most was the joy and the laughter. God was being so good, and I felt really pleased for Simon and John, who really didn't need to be there but had chosen to be, for me. A lot of healing was taking place. Even the Bay of Biscay behaved itself for once!

Back in Falmouth, the first thing we all did was pile into a good, old-fashioned English pub on the town quay for a piping hot Cornish pasty. We had anchored off the town and once again used our RIB, which by now had seen better days, to get ashore. The first people we saw were Colin and Diana, the people who gave us the RIB in the first place and who had sailed with us on the maiden voyage and beyond. They just happened to be on holiday. Colin was an ex Maritime and Coastguard Agency surveyor, and Diana a nurse. They had been such a blessing to us, and that RIB had been a lifeline to us—our only means of getting ashore when out at anchor—for the last ten years. I was reminded again of the sacrifice and generosity of so many who had made this project happen: people like Sue Witham, who did all the CCP administration in Grays all those years ago; Nigel and Olive Henderson, who bought us a portable generator to use at anchor; Tim and Jan, who let us use their home whenever we were in the UK; and all those who generously gave and prayed over the years. The list is endless. It was so humbling.

Back in the pub was a famous British actor, Steve McFadden, who plays Phil Mitchell in the British soap opera, *Eastenders*. He gave Sarah his autograph, as we all looked on bemused. It was very kind of him, but as we had been out of the country, we had never heard of him. I recalled how on the last day in the UK before we had sailed, a businessman had asked me for an auto-graph. I was embarrassed but impressed with his value system. In a few years' time, I would take my dad back to Normandy, where he had worked on the landing craft on D-Day. There on Pegasus Bridge we would witness French school kids getting the autographs of the retired British veterans. It was very impressive and why today I carry around an autograph book to ask some of the least likely celebrities, the older ones, perhaps invalids, to tell me their story and give me their autograph. It's so rewarding for me and a real blessing to them.

After a few days in Falmouth, we took on the very tricky navigation of the River Fal up to King Harry Ferry. It's a narrow, windy river that can be negotiated only at high water; and at the end of the trip, we had to turn the ship around so she was facing out again and moor to buoys. Once again, the only way ashore was by RIB.

Captain Alistair Sutherland was happy to stay aboard as watchman, and we moved back to London, where Sarah would shortly start school. John and Julie graciously let us stay with them at their home in Plumstead. We have fond memories of dropping Sarah off on her first day at Blackheath Bluecoats School and then taking Matt to pick up conkers in Greenwich Park. We really were back. Soon, we would realise that this was not a temporary thing. The Seacare project really was coming to an end, and the *Redeemer* would have to be sold off or preferably given to another ministry. Reluctantly, we would have to move quickly on this as the costs—port fees, insurance, fuel for the generator, etc.—would all continue even whilst she was laid up.

In the end we did find a buyer for the ship. Sadly, it was not another ministry, but eventually we were happy with the outcome, as she was bought by people who loved these old, Dutch pilot ships, and they restored her at great expense to her former glory. She is named *Castor* again and in the summer attends various maritime festivals. As I write this, John and Bernadette Pickering have recently returned from visiting her at her base in Rotterdam. The new owners have extended invites to myself and Adam in the States to actually sail on her. Neither of us has been able to yet, and personally I have mixed feelings about it, preferring, I think, to cling to my memories of her as the *Redeemer.* The new owners have a website and have respectfully included a whole section honouring us and our time on board. Readers can visit the website at http://www. loodsboot.eu/the_reedemer_years.htm.

Although St. Mildreds had been the church that sent us out and supported us so wonderfully, there had been many changes there over the ten years, with new leaders. Lots of the people who had supported us had moved on, so whilst obviously staying friends with those we knew at St. Mildreds, we chose to throw our lot in with the Ichthus Christian Fellowship. We had worked with Ichthus teams in Istanbul and Cyprus, and they had taken a lot of interest in us and supported me, in particular, pastorally during those years. So we moved back to Lee and joined a local congregation that I would eventually find myself leading. Ichthus is an amazing fellowship, cofounders of March for Jesus and so much more. They really have a heart for world missions, and even today, as I write this, thirty-two people from Ichthus have flown out to Thailand on outreach.

During this time my good friends Tony and Mary from Malta contacted us, except they were no longer in Malta but living in Preston in the northwest of England. They came down to see us in London, and Tony shared with me the devastating news that he had Motor Neurone Disease and may not have long to live. We were shocked. Tony was only forty years old and very fit. He loved to go diving in Grand Harbour, often around our ship, and sometimes he brought us the fish he had harpooned. This was such sad news.

We tried to organise a holiday for Tony and Mary in London, but he wasn't well enough to take it, so we went to visit them in Preston. I really had such a soft spot for this guy who had helped me out of trouble so often, and now I felt helpless. Of course I could pray and I did, but I have never understood the whole healing thing and why some are healed miraculously and others are not. I had believed God for the finances to run a ship project for ten years without fund-raising, but healing was another matter.

One day a few months later I suddenly felt the urge to ring Tony and Mary, so I did. Mary answered, "Oh Maurice, I am so glad you have called. Tony has gone into a coma, and we have sent for the priest to issue the last rites." As I put the phone down, I knew God was telling me to get into my car and go. It was the other end of the country, but I had to go.

When I got there, the priest was just leaving, and there was a lot of crying, obviously, and what sounded like wailing. The last rites had been ministered, and although Tony was alive, he wasn't expected to last long. I asked if I could be alone with Tony. Once I was alone with him and the bedroom door closed, I simply held his hand and started praying in the Spirit. What I didn't realise was that Mary had rigged up a children's intercom device, so everything I was saying was being relayed to the living room. Quietly and gently I explained to Tony how much God loved him (even though it didn't seem like that right now). I explained that Jesus had died on the cross for him and me and that all we needed to do was believe that and ask Him to come into our hearts as we choose to follow Him. If we do that and believe it, He will come; and when the time comes to die, we will be with Him for all eternity. I led Tony through this line by line and asked him to squeeze my hand after each sentence if he agreed and wanted to go on. God always gives us the dignity of choice! I believe I could feel that squeeze.

About half way through, the bedroom door opened, and Mary and her friend entered. I remember Mary's friend saying, "I don't know who you are or what's going on here, but I do know that a real peace has suddenly come over this household." That's all she said. The crying and everything had stopped, and I continued with my prayer. I believe with all my heart that Tony gave his life to the Lord at that moment. I returned to London the next morning.

Later that day I got a call from Mary. Tony had come out of his coma. Sadly, he was only to live another couple of days, but they were quality days, and he and Mary got to say their good-byes. Being a Catholic, Tony obviously would have a Catholic funeral in the local church presided over by the priest who gave him the last rites. So you can imagine how astonished I was when the invitation came to me to speak at the funeral. It was an honour of course, but also a very daunting prospect because I knew I would have to tell everyone about Tony's prayer and how we all need to say a prayer like that, and that, of course, would not fit in with some Catholic teaching. Would that be an impolite thing to do when they were graciously giving me this opportunity? But surely this was a message that had to be heard, and I would be failing the congregation if I didn't give it.

Furthermore, I learnt that a huge number of people would be coming over from Malta, including all the tough guys who drank in the pubs around the Three Cities area of Malta, where our ship had been berthed. These were people we had tried to reach for years. This was a final chance to share the good news with some precious souls, and I knew that now Tony would approve. So I went for it.

I think there must have been three hundred people in that church, with many standing. What a fitting tribute this was to a great guy. I said what I had to say, and the priest did "correct" me, and I understand why. Nevertheless, I don't regret it. People need to know that the Lord Jesus Christ died on the cross for them so that they can be reconciled to God and that the only way to do that is to invite the Lord Jesus Christ into their hearts and be born again. God so loved the world that He gave his only begotten son that whoever believed in him would not perish but have eternal life. (John 3 v16). Like Simeon, who had waited in the temple to embrace his salvation, so Tony had had his moment, and he too was now departing this world in peace; and I for one was very glad about that.

I drove home thanking God for the privilege of having Tony as a friend and for the opportunity to share the good news one final time with some of the wonderful Maltese people. But I knew now, that it was time to move on, the Seacare project really was well and truly over. Other opportunities and adventures would lie ahead.

We are not called to build our own organizations and empires, no matter how much we rationalize they are doing good. We are called to build the kingdom of God. We may feel weak and useless but it's about faith. The important thing is not what we can do for God, but what He can do through us if we have faith. *'Then they said to Him, "What shall we do, that we may work the works of God?" Jesus answered and said to them, "This is the work of God, that you believe......"* (John 6 v 28, 29)

FURTHER COPIES

If this book is not in your local Christian Bookshop, you should be able to order it.

It can also be purchased online at all the usual websites.

Multiple copies can be ordered by writing to:

CCP Trust
PO Box 24224, London
SE12 0ZW, England

(An invoice will be sent with the books.)

If you have any queries or would like to get in touch, we'd love to hear from you at:
vitsea1@aol.com

Lightning Source UK Ltd.
Milton Keynes UK
UKOW03f2347201113

221479UK00001B/1/P